PRESCHOOL BIBLE TREASURE LAND
Director Manual

TREASURE HUNT
Bible Adventure

Group
Loveland, Colorado

Preschool Bible Treasure Land Director Manual
Copyright © 1999 Group Publishing, Inc.

Credits
Treasure Hunt Bible Adventure Coordinator: Jody Brolsma
Author: Lori Haynes Niles
Chief Creative Officer: Joani Schultz
Copy Editor: Janis Sampson
Art Director: Kari K. Monson
Computer Graphic Artist: Randy Kady
Cover Art Director: Lisa Chandler
Cover Photographer: Craig DeMartino
Cover Designers: Becky Hawley and Jerry Krutar
Illustrators: Amy Bryant and Drew Rose
Rain Forest Art: Pat Allen
Rain Forest Art Photographer: Linda Bohm
Audio Engineer: Steve Saavedra
Production Manager: Peggy Naylor

ISBN 0-7644-9908-4
Printed in the United States of America.
10 9 8 7 6 5 4 3 2 1   00 99

CONTENTS

Welcome to TREASURE HUNT BIBLE ADVENTURE!

X marks the spot...for VBS excitement! Grab your compass, dust off your binoculars, and be sure your flashlight has batteries. You're hot on the trail to Treasure Hunt Bible Adventure, where kids discover Jesus—the greatest treasure of all! Your young adventurers will explore how the Bible maps the way to amazing riches, showing us the way to trust, love, pray, and live. Preschoolers begin each day's treasure hunt by doing fun motions to new as well as familiar Bible songs with the older kids at Sing & Play. Then they'll join with their Clue Crews to participate in age-appropriate, hands-on learning activities in Preschool Bible Treasure Land. Your little explorers will also get to experience "vine" dining at Treasure Treats, view *Chadder's Treasure Hunt Adventure* video, and join with older children each day for Treasure Time Finale!

Preschool Bible Treasure Land is a treasure-trove of hands-on Bible learning activities your preschoolers will love. Because the daily Bible Point is reinforced through a variety of activities that appeal to different learning styles, children keep discovering the riches of God's Word all day long! Check out the Treasure Hunt Bible Adventure Overview (pp. 10-11) to see how your Preschool Bible Treasure Land adventures connect with the older kids' expedition. The shaded columns describe activities that preschoolers will do with the entire VBS group. Then refer to the Treasure Land Schedule to see what your preschoolers will be doing each day.

Leading Preschool Bible Treasure Land is easy and fun!

You'll enjoy your role and be most successful as a Preschool Bible Treasure Land Leader if you

- ❧ enjoy working with small children;
- ❧ stock your room with blocks, dress-up clothes, modeling dough, and other age-appropriate toys and materials;
- ❧ get down on the floor and interact with children at their eye level;
- ❧ use simple language that preschoolers can understand; and
- ❧ model God's love in everything you say and do.

A CLUE FOR YOU!

Although it may be tempting to include everyone in VBS fun, we encourage you to use this program only with children who are *at least three years old*. Younger children tend to struggle with the structure and social setting of VBS programs.

A CLUE FOR YOU!

Although Clue Crew Leaders provide plenty of extra supervision for wiggly preschoolers, it's always a great idea to have an extra pair of hands to help keep your adventure under control. To make your job even easier, we highly recommend team leading. Leaders can alternate which days they prepare for or portions of each day they lead. For children ages three- to five-years-old, plan for one preschool leader for every twenty-five students; then build your staff from there!

- - - - - - - -

Field Test Findings

Our Preschool Bible Treasure Land adventures got off to a bumpy start because we had assigned middle-schoolers as Clue Crew Leaders. Although these kids were helpful and loving, they simply didn't have the initiative or know-how to lead preschoolers. By the end of the week, however, we had discovered that middle-schoolers make excellent assistant crew leaders!

Your Contribution to TREASURE HUNT BIBLE ADVENTURE

Here's what's expected of you before, during, and after Treasure Hunt Bible Adventure:

Before TREASURE HUNT BIBLE ADVENTURE

🍀 Attend scheduled Discovery Site Leader training.

🍀 Pray for the kids who will attend your church's Treasure Hunt Bible Adventure.

🍀 Ask your Treasure Hunt Director (otherwise known as your church's VBS Director) what you should wear each day. Discovery Site Leader T-shirts (available from Group Publishing and your local Christian bookstore) help kids identify you—and help you identify other Discovery Site Leaders. If your Treasure Hunt Director doesn't order T-shirts, you may want to agree on another easily recognizable uniform, such as tan shorts, explorer's vest, and hiking boots.

🍀 Read this Preschool Bible Treasure Land Director Manual. Each day's programming contains a variety of activities for you to choose from. You can set up all the activities or just a few—choose what works best for your class!

🍀 With your Treasure Hunt Director's help, recruit Clue Crew Leaders for your Preschool Bible Treasure Land. Clue Crew Leaders can be anyone from high school students to senior citizens. They need only to love the Lord and love children—and they don't have to prepare anything; they just help teach preschoolers by reinforcing the Bible Point throughout the day! You'll want to recruit one Clue Crew Leader for every three to five preschoolers. Middle school students make great Assistant Clue Crew Leaders.

🍀 After you've chosen crew leaders and assistant leaders, give crew leaders a Preschool Student Book for each preschooler in their crews. Clue Crew Leaders can keep the Student Books in their crews' treasure bags (available from Group Publishing and your local Christian bookstore) until children need them.

🍀 If Clue Crew Leaders can't come to your Discovery Site Leader training, distribute photocopies of the "For Clue Crew Leaders Only" handouts from the Treasure Hunt Director Manual (pp. 117-118). The handouts contain information to help Clue Crew Leaders succeed in their role at Treasure Hunt Bible Adventure.

You'll want to meet with the Clue Crew Leaders briefly to go over this information, answer their questions, and let them know about their special responsibilities as preschool helpers.

♣ Ask the Chadder's Treasure Hunt Theater Leader if you can preview the *Chadder's Treasure Hunt Adventure* video. Viewing the video before Treasure Hunt Bible Adventure will help you prepare children for what to watch for each day. Children will pay closer attention—and retain more—if they know what to watch for.

♣ Ask the Treasure Hunt Sing & Play Leader and the Treasure Time Finale Leader to reserve places up front for preschoolers each day. Label the seating area with a Preschool Bible Treasure Land sign or a flag. Preschoolers won't be able to read the sign, but older kids will.

♣ Use the clip art on the *Treasure Hunt Sing & Play Music & Clip Art CD* to create large signs for each Clue Crew. Name your Clue Crews after animals such as monkeys, jaguars, tree frogs, and snakes. Be sure to include clear pictures of the animals so nonreaders will be able to find their crews.

♣ Gather the supplies you'll need for the activities you've chosen.

♣ Designate a special area for preschoolers to be picked up each day. Tell the Treasure Time Finale Leader where you want preschoolers to gather at the end of the day.

During TREASURE HUNT BIBLE ADVENTURE

♣ Welcome children individually as they arrive. Let them know you're glad they've come to Treasure Hunt Bible Adventure. Keep in mind that some of the younger preschoolers may still feel anxious about leaving their parents or caregivers—your smiling, welcoming presence is important!

♣ Meet and greet each parent or caregiver. Encourage parents and caregivers to explore your room with their children. Explain that after Day 1, children may be dropped off in the Treasure Hunt Sing & Play area and that each day they may be picked up in your designated area. Reassure parents and caregivers that Clue Crew Leaders will stay with children until they're picked up.

♣ Help Clue Crew Leaders as they interact with preschoolers and reinforce the connection of the day's activities with the Point. Encourage Clue Crew Leaders to work closely with children so you can be free to travel among the Clue Crews.

♣ *On Day 1 only,* have preschoolers report directly to your Preschool Bible

A CLUE FOR YOU!

We can't say it enough—the volunteer training sessions really work! Encourage people to come in order to get a better understanding of their roles. It's an excellent way to prepare volunteers for the week ahead and to get them thinking (and praying) for children who will attend your program.

A CLUE FOR YOU!

It may be helpful to meet with the Treasure Hunt Director and go over the supply lists. Let the director know what supplies you have or can collect on your own and what supplies you'll need to purchase or collect from church members. You may want to photocopy each day's schedule and highlight the options you've chosen. Give the copy to your director so he or she can see what supplies you need each day. Open communication will make your job even easier!

Field Test Findings

In our Treasure Hunt Bible Adventure field test, we had over fifty preschoolers! Even though we had more children than we planned for, our preschool leaders survived...and actually enjoyed the week! We divided the class into two separate groups. One group participated in Chadder's Treasure Hunt Theater while the other was involved with the Bible Story Search Party. Then one group had fun with the Jungle Gym Playtime Activities, while the other traveled through the Rain Forest Exploration Stations. The whole group met together for snacks and Sing-Along Surprise.

Since preschoolers require so much more attention, consider placing only three children in each Clue Crew. If you're short on adult volunteers, place five preschoolers only in Clue Crews who have a crew leader and an assistant leader.

Treasure Land room after registration instead of going to the Treasure Hunt Sing & Play area. This will help children settle into their new surroundings before they prepare the snacks. Make sure you have some nondirected activities set up, such as blocks, dress-up, or modeling dough stations for the early arrivals.

♣ On Days 2 through 5, have preschoolers report directly to the Treasure Hunt Sing & Play area. Clue Crew Leaders can meet children at the door and, when everyone in their crews has arrived, lead them to the seating area set aside for them.

♣ To help create a fun atmosphere and reinforce Bible learning, play the *Treasure Hunt Sing & Play* audiocassette or CD as children enter and leave the Preschool Bible Treasure Land room.

♣ Tell the daily Bible story with expression and enthusiasm.

♣ Select and set up a variety of Rain Forest Exploration Stations and Jungle Gym Playtime Activities each day.

♣ On Day 1, help preschoolers prepare snacks for the entire Treasure Hunt Bible Adventure. This may sound impossible, but the Treasure Treats Leader will help you! Consult with him or her to determine whether to do this project in your preschool area or at the Treasure Treats area.

Children will learn important sharing and cooperation skills as they work together to create the snacks. And smiles will appear on every face when children realize their accomplishment.

♣ Accompany children when they leave the Preschool Bible Treasure Land room to go outside or join in other activities. Remind children to hold hands to keep everyone together.

♣ Consider incorporating some free-play time into your daily schedule. Most VBS programs last two to three hours, which is a long time for preschoolers to engage in structured programming. Check with the Jungle Gym leader to find out what Jungle Gym Gems are planned, and when preschoolers might be able to take advantage of these awesome extra activities!

♣ Have Clue Crew Leaders collect children's crafts and bring them to Treasure Time Finale (if the paint and glue are dry). If children have their crafts with them, parents and caregivers won't have to make an extra trip to your classroom.

♣ Repeat the daily Bible Point often. It's important to say the Point just as it's written. Repeating the Bible Point again and again will help children remember it and apply it to their lives. Whenever children hear the Bible Point, they'll respond by shouting "Eureka!" Each Preschool Bible Treasure Land activity suggests ways to include the Bible Point.

After **TREASURE HUNT BIBLE ADVENTURE**

♣ Return equipment to its proper place. Return the *Preschool Bible Treasure Land* audiocassette to your Treasure Hunt Director.

♣ Use the following ideas to remind children all year long about the treasures in God's Word:

♣ Phone neighborhood kids who participated in your Treasure Hunt Bible Adventure program;

○ Send Treasure Hunt Bible Adventure follow-up postcards;

○ Sing Preschool Bible Treasure Land songs, and repeat Rain Forest Exploration Stations or Jungle Gym Playtime Activities in Sunday school or midweek classes;

○ Show the *Chadder's Treasure Hunt Adventure* video in your Sunday school or midweek classes; and

○ Purchase a Chadder Chipmunk™ puppet for use with your preschool classes.

Field Test Findings

With more than fifty wiggly preschoolers, our leaders were more than apprehensive about the thought of preschoolers making the snack. "Can't you at least have them do it on a different day?" they asked. But those little ones pulled it off beautifully and were proud of their great accomplishment. Plus, it helped the entire VBS see that if preschoolers could do it— so could they!

Field Test Findings

We found that a rope fit in perfectly with the theme and allowed the preschoolers to have something to hold on to as they traveled. Some groups pretended they were carrying a giant slithering snake. Each preschooler was happy to do his or her part to see that the snake kept slithering all the way to the destination. Others became bumpy caterpillars or wiggly worms!

▼▼ TREASURE HUNT BIBLE ADVENTURE OVERVIEW ▼▼

This is what everyone else is doing! During Treasure Hunt Bible Adventure, the daily Bible Point is carefully integrated into each activity to reinforce Bible learning. Preschool Bible Treasure Land activities will fill most of your time.

	BIBLE POINT	BIBLE STORY	BIBLE VERSE	TREASURE HUNT SING & PLAY	CRAFT CAVE	JUNGLE GYM GAMES
DAY 1	The Bible shows us the way to trust.	Peter walks to Jesus on the Sea of Galilee (Matthew 14:22-33).	"Do not let your hearts be troubled. Trust in God" (John 14:1a).	● He's Got the Whole World in His Hands ● The B-I-B-L-E ● Where Do I Go? ● I've Found Me a Treasure (chorus and verse 1)	**Craft** Jungle Gel **Application** Kids need to trust the Craft Cave Leader that Jungle Gel really works. In the same way, we need to trust God when things in life seem impossible.	**Games** ● Swamp Squish ● Peter's Windy Walk ● The River Bend ● Treasure Tag ● Pass-Along Peter **Application** The Bible teaches us that God is powerful and that we can trust him.
DAY 2	The Bible shows us the way to love.	Jesus washes the disciples' feet (John 13:1-17).	"A new command I give you: Love one another" (John 13:34a).	● Put a Little Love in Your Heart ● I've Found Me a Treasure (add verse 2) ● Jesus Loves Me	**Craft** Operation Kid-to-Kid Magnetic Bible Bookmarks **Application** Just as the magnet links the two children on the bookmark together, the Bible connects us with others around the world.	**Games** ● Monkeys Love Bananas ● Footrace ● Gold Coin Keep-Away ● Firefly Fling ● Mosquito Net **Application** As the Bible shows us how to love, we can love others.
DAY 3	The Bible shows us the way to pray.	Jesus prays for his disciples and all believers, and then he is arrested (John 17:1–18:11).	"I pray also for those who will believe in me through their message, that all of them may be one" (John 17:20a-21b).	● Let Us Pray ● Hey Now ● I've Found Me a Treasure (add verse 3)	**Craft** Surprise Treasure Chests **Application** When kids open the treasure chest, they'll be surprised at the "riches" inside. When we open our hearts to God in prayer, we'll be surprised by his loving response.	**Games** ● Savor the Flavor ● Centipede Scurry ● Message Mime ● It's a Jungle! ● Flowers of Blessing **Application** It's easy to talk to God.
DAY 4	The Bible shows us the way to Jesus.	Jesus is crucified, rises again, and appears to Mary Magdalene (John 19:1–20:18).	"For God so loved the world that he gave his one and only Son, that whoever believes in him shall not perish but have eternal life" (John 3:16).	● He's Alive ● Make Your Home in My Heart ● Good News ● Oh, How I Love Jesus ● I've Found Me a Treasure (add verse 4)	**Craft** Good News Treasure Pouches **Application** The colorful beads on the Treasure Pouch will remind kids of the good news that Jesus died for our sins and rose again!	**Games** ● Roll Away the Stone ● Butterfly Breakout ● Manic Monarchs ● Jungle-Bird Jiggle ● He Has Risen! **Application** Our lives can be changed because Jesus rose from the dead.
DAY 5	The Bible shows us the way to live.	Paul stands firm in his faith, even in a shipwreck (Acts 27:1-44).	"If you love me, you will obey what I command" (John 14:15).	● The B-I-B-L-E ● Got a Reason for Livin' Again ● I've Found Me a Treasure (entire song)	**Craft** Rain Forest Creatures **Application** Kids add color and "life" to Rain Forest Creatures just as God's Word adds color and meaning to our lives.	**Games** ● Man-Overboard Tag ● Out to Sea ● Snake Swap ● Crash Course ● Cargo Toss **Application** Even when life seems scary or difficult, we can have confidence that God is in control.

This overview shows you what older kids will be doing. Your preschoolers will participate in the shaded activities. Be sure to check with your Treasure Hunt Director to see what time your little explorers will join the fun!

TREASURE TREATS	CHADDER'S TREASURE HUNT THEATER		BIBLE EXPLORATION	TREASURE TIME FINALE
Snack Peter's Adventure Cakes **Application** Peter's adventure began when he trusted Jesus. Jesus wants us to trust him, too.	**Video Segment** Chadder and his friends begin searching for a hidden treasure. They stumble onto the deck of the SS Hope, where Wally the parrot warns them to watch out for Riverboat Bob. Chadder's afraid, so Ryan, the first mate, tells him to trust God. The kids go to Whistle Cave, followed by Ned and Pete, two scraggly sailors who want the treasure for themselves. The kids find the treasure map, moments before they're trapped by a cave-in! **Application** ● Where do you turn when you're afraid? ● How does the Bible help you trust in God? ● Mark your Student Book at a Trust Verse.		**Peter Walks on Water** ● Experience being in a ship during a storm. ● Try walking on "water." ● Discuss how Peter learned to trust Jesus.	● Watch how a pin can go into a balloon, without popping the balloon! ● Use balloons to review the story of Peter walking on the water. ● Receive gem treasures as reminders that we are precious to God.
Snack Love Chests **Application** Jesus showed love for his disciples when he washed their feet. Today's snack shows that love is a great treasure.	**Video Segment** Chadder sits in an old mine car, and the car takes off, racing through the cave. Near the cave exit stands Riverboat Bob. He hits the hand brake and Chadder goes flying, right into the boxes Ryan has been stacking on deck. Chadder thinks Ryan will be mad, but Ryan says he follows Jesus' example of showing love. Chadder leaves to look for his friends, but runs into Riverboat Bob instead! **Application** ● Role play how you think Ryan will react to the mess Chadder made. ● How can the Bible help you when it's hard to love someone? ● How can the Love Verse you highlighted help you love this week?		**Jesus Washes the Disciples' Feet** ● Go on a barefoot hunt to find the Upper Room. ● Have their feet washed by their Clue Crew Leader. ● Help wash their Clue Crew Leader's feet. ● Help one another put their shoes back on.	● See how someone shows unexpected love to the Treasure Time Finale Leader. ● Receive heart locks and keys as treasures to remind them that loving actions open people's hearts.
Snack Prayer Treasure Mix **Application** Jesus' prayer teaches us to pray. The items in the Prayer Treasure Mix remind kids to pray about specific things.	**Video Segment** Chadder awakes in the mine and finds Hayley and Tim. They find a clue and decide to ask Ryan for help. The kids find Ryan in prayer, and Ryan shows them the Bible story of Jesus praying. Chadder wanders off, and Colonel Mike sees him and mistakes him for a scoundrel. Colonel Mike tells Chadder to walk the plank. **Application** ● Pray in your crew for the child who'll receive your Spanish Bible. ● Is there ever a time when you shouldn't pray? Explain. ● How can you pray as Jesus taught?		**Jesus Prays** ● Learn ways to pray for themselves. ● Practice praying for various groups of people. ● Create a mural with their hand prints to represent Jesus' prayer for all believers.	● Watch a skit about what it might be like for God to listen to our prayers. ● Receive magnifying glass treasures as reminders that prayer brings us closer to God.
Snack Empty Tombs **Application** On the third day, Jesus' tomb stood empty. These scrumptious snacks are empty, too.	**Video Segment** Ryan explains that Chadder's a friend, and Colonel Mike points the kids toward the monkey tree. Chadder loses the map, but Ryan assures him that Jesus is the real treasure. The wind blows the map back again, and the hunt continues. The kids find the treasure chest, and Chadder finds the key to the chest hidden in the old tree. Just as they open the chest, Ned and Pete step up to steal the treasure. **Application** ● How do you get to heaven? ● How can knowing the treasure of Jesus change your life? ● Why is it important to know about the treasure of Jesus?		**Mary Magdalene at the Empty Tomb** ● Experience the sadness of the crucifixion. ● Hear Mary tell how she searched for her lost treasure—Jesus—at the empty tomb. ● Hear "Jesus" call their names; then draw crosses on their mural hand prints to thank God for Jesus.	● Pray; then give their sins to "Jesus" and watch as he makes the sins disappear. ● Receive personal messages from their Clue Crew Leaders that Jesus loves them. ● Receive three gold coin treasures as reminders that Jesus is the most valuable treasure we have.
Snack Sailboat Sandwiches **Application** When Paul faced a shipwreck, his trust in God helped him. We can live an adventurous life when we believe in God.	**Video Segment** Ned and Pete plan to take the treasure, but Riverboat Bob steps in to help. Bob reveals that he's been watching over the kids all along. Colonel Mike wants to throw Ned and Pete to the alligators, but Ryan convinces him to show God's love. Hayley, Tim, and Chadder fantasize about what they'll do with the treasure, but decide to give the money to Colonel Mike to help him bring supplies and Bibles to people along the river. **Application** ● How can the Bible help you make decisions this week? ● What do you think about giving your Spanish Bible away? Why? ● When are times you can use the Bible verses you marked this week?		**Paul Is Shipwrecked** ● Be "handcuffed," and led inside a prisoner's ship. ● Hear a fellow prisoner tell about Paul's experience in the ship. ● Experience a shipwreck. ● Discuss how Paul's life was in God's control.	● Use a "chirping parrot" to experience the importance of working together to tell others about Jesus. ● Present their Spanish translations of the Gospel of John as a special offering. ● Receive a compass as a reminder that the Bible gives us direction in life.

GEARING UP FOR THE ADVENTURE!

Discovery Site Preparation

♣ Work with your Treasure Hunt Director to choose a room for Preschool Bible Treasure Land. You'll want a fairly large room that can remain set up all week. If your church has a preschool or kindergarten Sunday school room, see if you can use it.

♣ Make sure all furniture in your room is child-sized. If it's too big, it can cause accidents. If you can't get child-sized tables and chairs, remove the furniture and set up work areas on the floor. (Plastic tablecloths or even green trash bags taped to the floor work great for this because they denote special areas!)

♣ Plan for an eating area in your room. If you'll be using tables for other activities, you may want to have children eat on a plastic tablecloth on the floor.

♣ Stock your room with age-appropriate toys and games. In addition to the supplies listed on pages 14-15, children will enjoy dress-up clothes; animal masks; cardboard tubes to use as telescopes, periscopes, or binoculars; blocks; small suitcases or backpacks; modeling dough, toy food and dishes; dolls; and stuffed animals.

♣ Use the following suggestions to transform your room into a rain forest for Preschool Bible Treasure Land!

♣ Hang a net from the ceiling, and fill it with real or construction paper leaves to simulate a rain forest canopy. You can create a similar look with green yardage or even crepe paper! Drape and staple it about every three feet across the

ceiling. If you have a ceiling with acoustical tiles, you can lift the tiles and weave the fabric between the supports. Go the extra mile by cutting small slits in the fabric and pushing through twinkling white Christmas lights.

♣ Twist brown paper bags and staple on green construction paper leaves to create the liana of the rain forest. Attach these to the ceiling and drape them overhead. Add tissue paper flowers for variety. If you're lucky enough to have floor to ceiling supports in your room, be sure to wrap the "liana" around them too.

♣ Splatter-paint a canvas floor covering or large straw rug. Use different shades of brown and green paint to create a rain forest floor with a wonderful texture (while protecting the carpet!).

♣ Secure one or more carpet rolls to a wall with a liberal amount of duct tape. The carpet rolls can serve as giant tree trunks. You can also stabilize a carpet roll by placing it in front of a bulletin board and then securely attaching brown cotton broadcloth or canvas to the bulletin board on each side of the roll. Next, drill holes down the "trunk," and insert fabric or paper greenery into the holes.

♣ Consider replacing one or more of your regular light bulbs with a green light bulb to simulate the appearance of light coming through the trees (or make a green cellophane temporary light fixture). A rain forest floor is often almost dark because the canopy keeps the light from reaching it.

♣ Make life-size "shadow cutouts" of rain forest animals on black butcher paper. Hang these up on the walls so children can see how big they are in comparison to these animals. Are they as long as a leopard? tiny as a tree frog? giant as a gorilla? big as a boa? taller than a tapir?

♣ Paint egg-carton cups to resemble the noses or beaks of various rain forest animals. Attach elastic loops so that children can easily slip them on and off for dramatic play.

♣ Play the "Rain Forest Sounds" segment of the *1999 VBS: Skits & Drama* audiocassette.

♣ Mount an eye bolt in a ceiling beam to hang a rope from. Place pillows under the rope. Let preschoolers sit on the pillows and use the "vine" to pull themselves up to a standing position.

Field Test Findings

Preschoolers loved playing in the "jungle huts" made from large appliance boxes and grocery bags! Use the flaps of a box to create a peaked roof, and cut a window or two and a doorway. Then cover the whole structure with overlapping open grocery bags, secured only at the top of the bags. Cut each grocery bag into two-inch vertical strips, and curl the end of each strip around a pencil. A rubber snake will add the finishing touch. Fill the hut with stuffed rain forest animals for extra fun. Be sure to have more than one jungle hut—this will be a popular item!

A CLUE FOR YOU!

Many grocery stores and appliance stores give boxes away. Several weeks before your program begins, check with the stores in your area for the boxes you need to create your huts and caves.

Field Test Findings

We found that many of the week's projects had to be marked with names. We usually used masking tape for this purpose and stocked our Clue Crew treasure bags with a roll of tape and a permanent marker. However, you can save time by making computer-generated labels with each enrolled child's name pre-printed!

❧ Create a cave using a large appliance box. Make large crushed grocery-bag rocks to add texture to the inside and outside of the cave. A little spray glitter will create a treasure-rich effect, and a few jewels from the craft store will add to the excitement. Cover the mouth of the cave with green streamers so the preschoolers have to fight through the underbrush to get in. Cover part of the bottom of the box with an aluminum foil pool of water.

❧ Create snakes to hang around the room by stuffing the legs of green, black, or brown tights with cotton batting. If you want to keep the preschoolers from getting too close to a certain area, make a number of these and stitch them together to form a movable barrier.

❧ On Day 2, hang one of the "Operation Kid-to-Kid™" posters in your designated Chadder's Treasure Hunt Theater area. Then add a new poster on Days 3 and 4. These posters make the Bible project much more real and tangible to preschoolers who may not realize that kids around the world are a lot alike.

"Operation Kid-to-Kid™" posters are available from Group Publishing or your local Christian bookstore.

❧ Photocopy the "Preschool Bible Treasure Land" sign and arrow from the inside front and back covers of this manual. Place arrows along the church hallways leading to your room. Color the sign, and tape it on your meeting room door.

Preschool Bible Treasure Land Basic Supplies

Gather the basic supplies listed below, and then refer to the activities you've chosen to use to determine what other supplies you'll need. For a list of additional supplies (including supplies for each option), see pages 16-17.

○ a Bible
○ *Preschool Bible Treasure Land* audiocassette*
○ a cassette player
○ masking tape
○ transparent tape

○ paper
○ crayons
○ scissors
○ glue sticks
○ craft glue
○ paper towels
○ a bamboo whistle* or another attention-getting signal

Preschoolers will love visiting Chadder's Treasure Hunt Theater and watching Chadder Chipmunk! In fact, preschool children in previous Group VBS programs repeatedly asked their leaders, "When is Chadder Chipmunk coming to our room?" If you want to add extra fun to your Preschool Bible Treasure Land, purchase a Chadder Chipmunk puppet from Group Publishing or your local Christian bookstore. You can also purchase a pattern to make a life-size Chadder costume! Use the following ideas to incorporate Chadder Chipmunk into your daily activities.

● Have Chadder Chipmunk welcome preschoolers as they arrive.
● Have Chadder Chipmunk sing Treasure Hunt Bible Adventure songs with children.
● Have Chadder Chipmunk blow your bamboo whistle (with your help).
● Have Chadder Chipmunk participate in games.
● Have Chadder Chipmunk ask children questions about the Bible Point or the Bible story.

A CLUE FOR YOU!

Attention-getting signals let children know when it's time to stop what they're doing and look at you. You can use the bamboo whistle (available from Group Publishing or your local Christian bookstore) or another noisemaker of your choice. The first time students come to the Preschool Bible Treasure Land, introduce and rehearse your attention-getting signal. Once children are familiar with the signal, regaining their attention will become automatic.

Discovery Site Safety Tips

♣ Remove any small toys or objects that children could swallow or choke on. It's wise to remove anything smaller than a fifty-cent piece.

♣ If you take children outdoors, keep them within a confined area. If your church doesn't have a fenced-in area, you may want to mark off an area with a rope border.

♣ Make sure all children are holding hands before you leave your room. This will help them stay together. You might want to provide a rope for each Clue Crew. Children can hold tightly to sections of the rope, while their Clue Crew Leader holds one end of it.

♣ Release preschoolers only to parents or caregivers after Treasure Hunt Bible Adventure each day to ensure that children don't get lost.

Field Test Findings

We found our attention-getting signal worked best by having the class respond to the signal with a "rain forest hush." Both children and adults stopped, put their fingers to their lips, whispered "shh," and listened for the tiniest sounds of the rain forest. It almost sounded like real rain!

Additional Supplies

Use this page as a checklist as you stock your Preschool Bible Treasure Land with supplies. **Depending upon the options you choose, you may not need all the supplies listed below.**

Things you can find at home

- ○ three bedsheets or towels or other simple supplies for Bible-time costumes
- ○ a flat bedsheet (preferably blue)
- ○ five inner tubes or blow-up swim tubes
- ○ small toys or kitchen items to sink and float
- ○ three cinder blocks
- ○ a bath towel
- ○ a Crock-Pot with savory-smelling contents (optional)
- ○ a bucket
- ○ dishwashing soap (Joy liquid works best.)
- ○ plastic wrap

- ○ wax paper
- ○ two to four paintbrushes
- ○ Bubble Wrap scraps
- ○ two gift-wrapped boxes
- ○ a mirror
- ○ a broomstick
- ○ fabric scraps
- ○ an old garden hose
- ○ two funnels
- ○ spray bottles filled with water
- ○ blue food coloring
- ○ facial tissues
- ○ a plastic outdoor garbage can (clean and disinfected that can be cut apart)
- ○ a box of cereal

Things you can find at church

- ○ blocks
- ○ a flashlight
- ○ permanent markers
- ○ paper cups
- ○ craft sticks
- ○ blue finger paint
- ○ balls and other outdoor play equipment
- ○ duct tape
- ○ scented baby lotion

- ○ toy housekeeping items
- ○ baby wipes
- ○ bubble solution
- ○ plastic gloves
- ○ newsprint or butcher paper
- ○ yarn
- ○ black chenille wires
- ○ watercolor markers
- ○ cotton balls

Field Test Findings

We encourage you to use Group's Rain Forest Seeds because they grow in as few as five days! Children will love watching the seeds grow in their Mini Rain Forests!

Things you need to purchase or collect

- ○ Treasure Hunt Bible Adventure name badges*
- ○ Treasure Hunt sticker sheets: Preschool*
- ○ Preschool Student Books*

- ○ Gel Cells*
- ○ Rain Forest Seeds*
- ○ Mini Jungle Vine*
- ○ Good News Treasure Pouches*
- ○ two children's wading pools

○ Operation Kid-to-Kid Magnetic Bookmarks*
○ three eight-foot two-by-fours
○ a 4x8-foot sheet of Masonite or heavy cardboard
○ gel glue
○ liquid laundry starch
○ dark-colored socks (one per child)
○ wire clothes hangers
○ resealable plastic snack bags (Use Glad bags only—or you'll have lots of leaks!)

○ craft foam hearts
○ sponge paintbrushes
○ red fabric paint or acrylic paint
○ white washcloths (one per child)
○ Surprise Treasure Chest Kit*
○ glue-on gems and sequins
○ two-liter plastic soda bottles (one per child)
○ potting soil
○ Hershey's Kisses candies or gold-wrapped chocolate coins
○ Ping-Pong balls

A CLUE FOR YOU!

We recommend that you use the Treasure Hunt sticker sheets, rather than trying to find stickers on your own. Each Treasure Hunt sticker sheet has all the stickers one child needs for the entire week. What a time saver!

- - - - - - - -

*These items are available from Group Publishing or your local Christian bookstore.

WHAT'S A CLUE CREW?

Clue Crews are small groups of preschoolers that participate in Rain Forest Exploration Stations together each day. They also hold hands (or ropes) when they travel outside the Preschool Bible Treasure Land. Each Clue Crew consists of up to five children and one adult or teenage Clue Crew Leader. With one leader shepherding five children, you can be assured your preschoolers will get lots of attention...and discipline issues diminish! Depending on the size and age mix of your church's Treasure Hunt Bible Adventure, each Clue Crew may include children ages three, four, and five. Use the developmental information below to guide you as you work with preschoolers at your Treasure Hunt Bible Adventure.

A CLUE FOR YOU!

Clue Crew Leaders will have a much easier time if you include three-, four-, and five-year-olds in each group. Four- and five-year-olds will be able to do many of the activities themselves, leaving the Clue Crew Leaders free to help the three-year-olds. Clue Crews will also be able to finish activities in about the same amount of time.

We're three years old. We've just learned how to really play together. We like playing with others, but we're still learning how to share and take turns. It also may be a little hard for us to change activities, so give us plenty of warning ahead of time. When we don't respond as quickly as you think we should, we're not being uncooperative, it just takes us a moment to shift gears.

We're generally happy and sometimes even silly, but we may be a little shy about trying new things. We enjoy playing games that involve moving and jumping around, but we may tire more quickly than our older playmates.

We'll probably need a little grown-up help to complete some of the Treasure Hunt Bible Adventure activities, especially those that involve squeezing glue or cutting.

We're ready to discover Jesus at Treasure Hunt Bible Adventure!

We're four years old. We're full of imagination and excitement. We love to use our imaginations in pretend play and art activities.

We like to use loud voices and big movements. You may need to remind us to play quietly in the Preschool Bible Treasure Land.

We enjoy listening to Bible stories and answering interesting questions such as "What do you think it was like to sail on a ship?"

We're ready to discover Jesus at Treasure Hunt Bible Adventure!

We're five years old. We love to help our Clue Crew Leaders and our Preschool Bible Treasure Land Leader. If you notice us helping, please say, "Thank you."

We're proud of the things we can do, but we're also sensitive. Other children may hurt our feelings by blurting out reactions to things we do.

We're growing in coordination. We can cut with scissors and color between the lines. We're also pretty good at throwing and catching balls.

We're ready to discover Jesus at Treasure Hunt Bible Adventure!

WHAT'S OPERATION KID-TO-KID™?

More Than an Offering

In developing Treasure Hunt Bible Adventure, the VBS team at Group Publishing wanted to include a meaningful service project that would help kids realize that with God's help, even children can impact the world! From customer feedback, we learned that VBS Directors (like you) wanted kids to give more than money. They wanted kids to give something that was meaningful and tangible—something that would meet the needs of children across the world.

We met with International Bible Society, an organization with a heart for reaching people with God's Word. Their partnerships with other Bible translators have resulted in the publication of 166 New Testaments and 1,283 Scripture publications in 506 languages. IBS places Bibles in the hands of millions, from every corner of the world! When we approached their staff and talked about working together, IBS caught the vision and joined Operation Kid-to-Kid.

How Your Kids Can Help

Each child will find a Spanish translation of the Gospel of John in his or her Student Book. During the week, kids will highlight and mark key passages in their own Bible books as well as in the Spanish Bible books. In Preschool Bible Treasure Land, kids will each create a fun Operation Kid-to-Kid Magnetic Bookmark. Aside from being useful and fun, the bookmark shows how the Bible draws us together even when distance or language barriers keep us apart. Kids place the bookmarks at Juan 3:16; then they present the Spanish Bible books as an offering during the last Treasure Time Finale.

Field Test Findings

Many of our VBS customers told us that they wanted to incorporate a missions project in their own area. With Operation Kid-to-Kid, it's a snap! If you live in or near a Spanish-speaking community, let the kids in your program distribute the Gospels of John themselves. If your church supports a missionary in a Spanish-speaking country, ship the books to the missionary for distribution. Feel free to personalize this project to make it most meaningful for your church!

Specifics (This is the easy part!)

Inside each child's Student Book, you'll find a Spanish translation of the Gospel of John. This is our way of partnering with you to make Operation Kid-to-Kid happen! The Craft Cave Leader and Preschool Bible Treasure Land Leaders will explain Operation Kid-to-Kid on Day 2. Then, during Treasure Hunt Bible Adventure, kids will use simple stickers and highlighters to mark key Bible passages that will help Spanish-speaking children better understand God's Word. Kids will also create clever Operation Kid-to-Kid Magnetic Bookmarks to include in their Spanish translations, as additional gifts to Spanish-speaking children.

On Day 5, kids will detach the Spanish translations from their Student Books. Then kids will present the books during a special Treasure Time Finale. After VBS is over, place the books in a box and seal it up. Affix the mailing label found in the Operation Kid-to-Kid brochure; then ship the books to IBS. They'll send the books to their international offices in Spanish-speaking countries for distribution. It's that easy!

Thanks for joining us in this exciting, world-changing project!

DAY 1

BIBLE POINT

The Bible shows us the way to trust.

BIBLE BASIS

Matthew 14:22-33. Peter walks to Jesus on the Sea of Galilee.

When Jesus called, "Come, follow me," Peter didn't hesitate to abandon his fishing nets in obedience. As Jesus' disciple, Peter listened to Jesus' teachings, watched Jesus heal the sick, and witnessed Jesus' power over wind and waves. He believed that Jesus was the Son of God. Perhaps that's why, on the stormy Sea of Galilee, when Jesus said, "Come," Peter ventured from the safety of a boat and walked toward Jesus. The water may have been cold, the waves may have been high, and the wind may have stung his face, but Peter knew that the safest place to be was with Jesus. When Peter became afraid and began to sink, "Immediately, Jesus reached out his hand and caught him." In the arms of Jesus, Peter learned to trust. He later wrote, "Cast all your anxiety on him because he cares for you" (1 Peter 5:7).

The disciple Peter is the perfect picture of our humanity and weakness; he reminds us how desperately we need Jesus. Children feel that need just as keenly as adults. They're familiar with the fear that accompanies life's "storms"—when parents divorce, friends move away, pets die, and classmates tease. The children at your VBS need to know that, in the midst of those hard times, Jesus is calling them to "come." And when children step out in faith, Jesus will be there with open arms, ready to catch them. Today's activities will encourage children to cast all their worries upon a loving, compassionate, and mighty God.

Customize your Preschool Bible Treasure Land activities to fit your schedule and facilities. Follow these steps for a fantastic, fun-filled preschool program each day.

● Consult with your Treasure Hunt Director to find out where Chadder's Treasure Hunt Theater and Treasure Time Finale will be meeting. Fill in these locations on the Treasure Land Schedule.

● Determine with your Treasure Hunt Director where to hold Jungle Gym Playtime Activities. Fill in this location on the Treasure Land Schedule.

● Choose which Rain Forest Exploration Stations you'll use, and collect the supplies you'll need.

● Choose which Jungle Gym Playtime Activities options you'll use, and collect the supplies you'll need.

● Choose which Sing-Along Surprise songs you'll use, and cue the *Preschool Bible Treasure Land* audiocassette to the first song you've chosen.

● Determine with the Jungle Gym Games Leader whether or not children can visit a Jungle Gym Gem today, and what time it will be available for preschoolers.

A CLUE FOR YOU!

If you have more than two hundred (elementary and preschool) children at your VBS, you may want preschoolers to place their crafts and Student Books in a special area of your room. Make copies of the Clue Crew animal signs, and post them along one wall in the Preschool Bible Treasure Land room. After Treasure Time Finale, preschoolers can return to the room and wait to be picked up near their animal signs.

TREASURE LAND SCHEDULE

LOCATION	ACTIVITY	MINUTES	WHAT CHILDREN WILL DO	CLASSROOM SUPPLIES	PRESCHOOL STUDENT BOOK SUPPLIES
Preschool Bible Treasure Land	Report for Adventure!	up to 10	Meet their classmates and Clue Crew Leaders, and practice the attention-getting signal.	Treasure Hunt Bible Adventure name badges, permanent markers, "Bible Point" posters	
	Treasure Treats Service	up to 25	Make Peter's Adventure Cakes and learn that the Bible shows us the way to trust.	Supplies provided by Treasure Treats Leader	
Preschool Bible Treasure Land	Bible Story Search Party	up to 15	Hear about Peter and Jesus' adventure walking on the water and learn that the Bible shows us the way to trust.	Bible, blue sheet, a flashlight, an extra sheet or a Bible costume, and a helper to be Jesus	
Preschool Bible Treasure Land	Rain Forest Exploration Stations	up to 20	**Option 1: Mini Rain Forests**—Make a miniature rain forest in a bottle.	Empty 2-liter bottles (cut in half), potting soil, rain forest seeds, water	
			Option 2: A Block Sea—Construct a large flat sea and act out the Bible story.	Blocks	
			Option 3: Jungle Gel Necklaces—Make a special gel to experience trust.	Gel glue, liquid starch, craft sticks, plastic spoons, paper cups, paper towels, Mini Jungle Vine, Gel Cells, Treasure Hunt sticker sheets	
			Option 4: Peter's Water-Walk Theater—Create a personal puppet stage to review the Bible story.	Blue finger paint, fine-point permanent marker, baby wipes, Treasure Hunt sticker sheets	Treasure Land Activity Page: Day 1
	Chadder's Treasure Hunt Theater	up to 15	Hear how Chadder Chipmunk goes on a treasure hunt and gets lost.	Supplies provided by Chadder's Treasure Hunt Theater Leader, Treasure Hunt sticker sheets	Preschool Student Books (p. 2-3)
Preschool Bible Treasure Land	Treasure Treats	up to 15	Eat Peter's Adventure Cakes and get to know their Clue Crews.	Snacks made earlier, paper towels, crayons	Preschool Student Books (p. 1)
	Jungle Gym Playtime Activities	up to 20	**Option 1: Hand-to-Hand Relay**—Learn about trust by taking a "blind" walk with a friend.		
			Option 2: Rain Forest Ramp Run—Slide down the ramp on "rain forest leaves" and learn to trust their leaders.	Masonite, three cinder blocks, three two-by-fours, wax paper	
			Option 3: Riverboat Rides—Push and pull each other in inner tube "boats."	Inner tubes, duct tape, crew ropes	
			Option 4: Free Play—Enjoy free play outdoors or in the classroom.	Playground equipment, classroom toys	
Preschool Bible Treasure Land	Sing-Along Surprise	up to 15	Sing Bible action songs.	Bible, treasure box, cassette player, *Preschool Bible Treasure Land* audiocassette: "The B-I-B-L-E," "I've Found Me a Treasure"	
	Treasure Time Finale	up to 20	Use balloons to celebrate the fact that we can trust Jesus.	Supplies provided by Treasure Time Finale Leader	

Preschool Bible Treasure Land Prep

Before children arrive:

● Consult with the Treasure Treats Leader about how preschoolers will prepare today's snacks. Agree on a place (your room or the Treasure Treats area) and a time to prepare the snacks. Ask the Treasure Treats Leader how you and your Clue Crew Leaders can help during snack preparation. If necessary, set up a snack-preparation area in your room.

● Set up the Rain Forest Exploration Stations you've selected. If you choose to create the Mini Rain Forests, cut all the bottles in half. It's a good idea to make a Mini Rain Forest ahead of time so children can see what they'll be making. Also set out blocks, stuffed animals, or other classroom toys for children to play with if they arrive early.

● Remember that preschoolers will be spending their opening time in the Preschool Bible Treasure Land today rather than attending Treasure Hunt Sing & Play. This will allow time for children to meet their Clue Crew Leaders and will ensure that you'll be ready for Treasure Treats Service. On Days 2 through 5, you and your Clue Crew Leaders will meet preschoolers in the Treasure Hunt Sing & Play area.

● Get registration materials from your Treasure Hunt Director. He or she will have preregistered preschoolers and put them into Clue Crews. Be sure to get extra forms for any walk-in registration needs.

● Give each crew leader and assistant leader a large sign with their crew name and a picture of that animal on it. Have Clue Crew Leaders wait in the Preschool Bible Treasure Land area, holding up their signs so parents and other caregivers can see them.

● Give five Treasure Hunt Bible Adventure name badges, a roll of masking tape, a permanent marker, and five Preschool Student Books to each Clue Crew Leader. Clue Crew Leaders can place the items in their crew treasure bags.

Report for Adventure!

(up to 10 minutes)

When children arrive, greet each child individually with an enthusiastic smile. Point out or lead the child to his or her Clue Crew Leader. As you greet children, ask them their names. Have Clue Crew Leaders write each child's name on a name badge and the crew sign.

Tell children you're glad they've come to visit Treasure Hunt Bible Adventure, and then invite them to play with the toys you've set out.

When everyone has arrived, have Clue Crew Leaders help children put away the toys and then join you on the floor. Be sure children are sitting with their Clue Crews.

Say: **Hello, everybody! Welcome to Treasure Hunt Bible Adventure!**

A CLUE FOR YOU!

Check with your Treasure Hunt Director to be sure he or she recruited a helper for preschool registration. Let the helper check in children so you can be available to greet and guide children to their Clue Crew Leaders. *Communication with your registration workers, Clue Crew Leaders, and Assistant Clue Crew Leaders is essential for getting off to a good start.* Make sure you have a fool-proof plan to make preschoolers and their caretakers feel welcome and safe.

Field Test Findings

In our field test, we found that this one-on-one connection was a great start to the week. Plus, it gave the parents a chance to meet the Clue Crew Leaders...then they knew who their children were gushing about all week!

Field Test Findings

Within minutes of arrival time at our field test, we had one child become ill and one with serious separation anxiety. We quickly learned to back up our registration and arrival plans with a "Plan B" and lots of extra help!

BIBLE POINT
BIBLE POINT

A CLUE FOR YOU!

You'll probably need a volunteer to staff the registration table for fifteen to twenty minutes after your program begins to assist latecomers. Have the volunteer walk each child inside and help him or her find the right Clue Crew.

We're going to have a great time together this week. Every day this week when you come to Treasure Hunt Bible Adventure, we're going to pretend this whole building is a huge rain forest, filled with hidden treasures and lots of exciting creatures like monkeys, tree frogs, jaguars, and bugs.

Let's make some big monkey ears! Pull your ears out to the side to demonstrate.

Let's make some crocodile jaws. Extend both arms in front of you, palms together.

Let's crawl some creepy little bugs up our arms. Walk your fingers up your arm.

Continue: **Before explorers can go on treasure hunts, they have to learn some rules for safe traveling and how to use some tools to help them along their journey. Just as all explorers need maps to guide them, at Treasure Hunt Bible Adventure we need a map. We'll have fun and play games while we learn about God's special treasure map, the Bible. The Bible shows us the way to all kinds of wonderful treasures. Today we're learning that ❀ the Bible shows us the way to trust. Each time you hear someone say ❀ the Bible shows us the way to trust, you can shout "Eureka!" "Eureka" means "I found something special!" So keep your ears open and shout "Eureka!" each time you hear the Bible Point!**

There's something special we can do to stay together as we travel around and have adventures at Treasure Hunt Bible Adventure. Whenever we leave our room, we'll hold each other's hands so we can all stay together.

While you're here in our Preschool Bible Treasure Land, you'll be with a group of other children in a Clue Crew. Sometimes we'll all do the same thing together, and sometimes your Clue Crew will get to do special things all by yourselves.

Each Clue Crew will have a Clue Crew Leader. Let's have all the Clue Crew Leaders stand up. You can tell Clue Crew Leaders by the special hats they wear.

Introduce each Clue Crew Leader to children. Then continue: **If you need help with anything, your Clue Crew Leader will help you. Now take a minute to meet the other explorers in your crew.**

Have Clue Crew Leaders lead their Clue Crews in getting acquainted. After a couple of minutes, blow two short blasts on the bamboo whistle and say: **Attention, everyone! This is our bamboo whistle.** Blow the bamboo whistle again. **Bamboo whistles get people's attention. When I blow my bamboo whistle once** (demonstrate), **it means I need your attention. If I blow my bamboo whistle twice like this** (blow whistle two times), **it means I want you to find your Clue Crew and stand together.**

Let's play a game to practice that. We'll all move around the room and pretend we're walking through the rain forest. When I blow the bamboo whistle two times, find your Clue Crew members and join hands. Ready? Let's begin.

As you move around the room with children, pretend to be walking through a rain forest. After about fifteen seconds, blow the bamboo whistle two times, and wait while children assemble in their crews.

When all the Clue Crews have assembled, say: **You did a great job forming your Clue Crews! Let's practice that one more time.**

Repeat the exercise. Then say: **I'm so proud of how quickly you can find your Clue Crews and hold hands! Now let's all get ready to begin our Treasure Hunt Bible Adventure.**

Treasure Treats Service

(up to 25 minutes)

Today preschoolers will prepare snacks for the entire Treasure Hunt Bible Adventure. If you've decided to prepare the snacks in your classroom, the Treasure Treats Leader will come and help preschoolers complete this project. If the Treasure Treats Leader hasn't arrived yet, send a Clue Crew Leader to the Treasure Treats area to let the Treasure Treats Leader know you're ready. If you've arranged for preschoolers to go to the Treasure Treats area to prepare the snack, send a Clue Crew Leader ahead to tell the Treasure Treats Leader you're coming. When the Clue Crew Leader returns, have children gather in their Clue Crews and hold hands as they travel to the Treasure Treats area.

When you're ready to prepare the snacks, say: **Attention, Clue Crews! I'd like you to meet** [name of Treasure Treats Leader], **our Treasure Treats Leader.** [Name] **is going to help us make some yummy treats that we can share with everyone at Treasure Hunt Bible Adventure!**

After you've introduced the Treasure Treats Leader, he or she will tell children about the snack they'll be making, have children wash their hands, and then help them prepare the snacks. The Treasure Treats Leader will assign specific preparation tasks to children and Clue Crew Leaders.

After children have prepared the snacks, set aside enough snacks for your class. Be sure to take water, cups, and napkins, too. The Treasure Treats Leader will serve the rest of the snacks to older children later in the day. If you have plenty of Clue Crew Leaders, have one or two help the Treasure Treats Leader transport the snacks to serving tables. Have the remaining Clue Crew Leaders use wet cloths to help you clean the snack preparation area—and children!

When everyone is cleaned up and all your Clue Crew Leaders are finished with their tasks, blow the bamboo whistle two times, and help children gather in their Clue Crews. Say: **Good job finding your Clue Crews—and good job making those snacks! We'll get to eat our snacks a little bit later. Right now, we're going to do some other fun things, starting with our**

Bible Story Search Party! Remember to stay with the members of your Clue Crew as we head that direction.

Bible Story Search Party

(up to 15 minutes)

Before the story, lay the big blue bedsheet in the center of the floor. Have a helper prepared to walk into the room dressed as Jesus. When he enters the room, he should be carrying a flashlight and have it shining on his face. This person's only responsibility will be to stand at one end of the sheet and reach out a hand to help children walk across the "lake."

Have children gather around the sheet. Let each child hold an edge and shake the sheet. Ask:

● **What does this big wavy sheet waving remind you of?** (Water; our swimming pool.)

● **Think about a time you have been around water. Were you at a lake or an ocean or a swimming pool? What was it like?** (Wet; cold; fun; scary.)

Have children set the sheet down, and ask them each to make a boat-shape by cupping their hands together.

Open your Bible to Matthew 14:22-33, and show the passage to the children. Say: **Our Bible story for today took place in a boat** (hold out your cupped hands) **on the sea.** Place your cupped hands on the edge of the sheet, and encourage children to follow your lead. **It was late at night and it was dark.** Have a Clue Crew Leader turn off the lights in the room. **Jesus sent his friends to a boat; he walked up a mountain to pray by himself.**

The boat drifted farther and farther from shore, and the waves rocked the boat from side to side. Have children shake the sheet again. **Soon, in the distance, Jesus' friends noticed something strange.** Have your Jesus character enter at this point. **They noticed it was coming closer and closer to their boat, and they were afraid. Then Jesus' friends figured out it was a person, and they heard him say, "Don't be afraid." They knew then that it was Jesus. But how could Jesus be walking on the water toward them?** Have children hold the sheet still. Ask:

● **What happens when you step into the bathtub?** (My foot hits the bottom; it makes a splash.)

● **What happens when you step in a puddle?** (My shoe gets wet; I splash my mom.)

● **What happens when you step into a swimming pool or a lake?** (I get all wet; my legs get wet; my feet touch the sand.)

Say: **Jesus wasn't swimming to the boat. He was walking on top of the water! None of us can do that! But Peter said: "If it's you, Jesus, let me walk out to you!" Jesus told Peter to come on out of the boat.** Step onto the blue sheet while encouraging children to continue making waves.

A CLUE FOR YOU!

For the first day or two, you'll need to prompt preschoolers to shout "Eureka!" whenever they hear the Bible Point. By the third day, they will have caught on wonderfully!

- - - - - - -

Start walking toward "Jesus." Then look down at your feet and the waves around you, and pretend to start sinking. Say: **Help me, Jesus!** Reach out your hand toward "Jesus," and walk all the way to the other side of the sheet. Ask children if they would like to pretend to be Peter walking out on the water to Jesus.

Allow one crew at a time to stand. Then let each member from the crew walk across the sheet while the other crews continue to make waves. As each child steps on to the sheet, have the whole group say together, "Keep your eyes on 'Jesus'!" The children will find that it's difficult to walk to "Jesus" if they're looking at the waves around them. If a child looks as though he or she might fall, have "Jesus" reach across the waves to offer a hand, or encourage a Clue Crew Leader to walk with the child. When everyone who wants to has walked across the sheet, ask:

● **How did you feel when you were walking on the water?** (Funny; a little scared; weird.)

● **What helped you get across our pretend sea?** ("Jesus" was there to catch me; my Clue Crew Leader helped; I knew it wasn't dangerous.)

● **When have you been afraid of a storm or something else that was scary?** Answers will vary.

Say: **Peter was frightened. He had to trust Jesus to help him get safely inside the boat. We trust Jesus to help us when we are frightened and need help.** ⊛ **The Bible shows us the way to trust** (Eureka!), **just as Peter trusted Jesus.**

We also have other special helpers we can trust, like our Clue Crew Leaders. Whenever you're afraid or need help this week, your Clue Crew Leader will be right there to help you.

Teach children this chant that can be repeated frequently during the day.
[Crew name, crew name],
One, two, three. *(Count with fingers.)*
We trust Jesus. *(Point up.)*
Way to be! *(Give thumbs up sign.)*

Rain Forest Exploration Stations
(up to 20 minutes)

Because the Rain Forest Exploration Stations all build on the lesson your children learned during Bible Story Search Party, encourage your Clue Crew Leaders to involve their Clue Crews in as many options as possible.

X

⊛ **BIBLE POINT**

A CLUE FOR YOU!

To be sure children are "with you" during the story, you may want to stop occasionally and ask factual questions such as "Who was walking on the water?" or "Where was Jesus?"

A CLUE FOR YOU!

Before class each day, choose and set up several or all of the Rain Forest Exploration Stations. If you're using the same room for the Bible story and the activities, you may want to cover up the activity work areas with plastic tablecloths or bedsheets to keep children's attention focused on you until you're ready for the activities to begin.

Photocopy and cut out the instructions for each day's Rain Forest Exploration Stations. Place a copy of the appropriate instructions near each station. Clue Crew Leaders can read the instructions and help children complete the activities.

If the children in your class are too young to stay in structured groups for very long, you may want to station one Clue Crew Leader at each station and let children move from station to station individually.

You may want to include an additional station each day that is equipped with a cassette player and the *Preschool Bible Treasure Land* audiocassette. Children can sing and dance with the music.

RAIN FOREST EXPLORATION STATIONS

▼▼ Option 1: MINI RAIN FORESTS ▼▼▼▼▼▼▼▼▼▼▼▼

1. Show children the sample Mini Rain Forest.

2. Let each child scoop up some potting soil with the bottom portion of his or her soda bottle. Demonstrate how to make a hole in the center of the soil.

3. Give each child at least two or three Rain Forest Seeds to drop into the hole, and then let him or her cover the seeds with a small handful of potting soil. Have each child pour no more than one-eighth cup of water on the soil.

4. Point out how the water has condensed (or made little "rain-drops") around the inside of the sample rain forest.

5. Say: **In this little rain forest, God will take care of the seeds and help them to grow into plants.** ✿ **The Bible shows us the way to trust.** (Eureka!) **We can trust that God will take care of us and help us grow, too! As you watch your seeds grow, you can remember to trust God!**

6. Write each child's name on the top portion of his or her soda bottle; then help children place the soda bottle top over the bottom. Be sure they pick up and hold the Mini Rain Forest bottles from the bottom so that they don't come apart.

A CLUE FOR YOU!

To achieve authentic-looking Mini Rain Forests, set the finished projects in a sunny area. Children (and adults!) will be amazed to see the special Rain Forest Seeds grow in just five days! Children can take home their Mini Rain Forests on Day 5.

▼▼ Option 2: A BLOCK SEA ▼▼▼▼▼▼▼▼▼▼▼▼▼▼▼

1. Have children use blocks to build a flat sea and then use other blocks to be ships on the sea.

2. Let children walk on their block sea, pretending to be Peter.

3. As children work and play, review the story of Peter walking out to Jesus. Point out that ✿ the Bible shows us the way to trust and we can always go to Jesus because he loves us.

RAIN FOREST EXPLORATION STATIONS

▼▼ Option 3: JUNGLE GEL NECKLACES ▼▼▼▼▼▼▼

1. Give one cup and one craft stick to each child.

2. Measure one plastic spoonful of liquid starch and one level spoonful of gel glue into each cup.

3. Have preschoolers use craft sticks to stir and "smoosh" the mixture. Say: ✸ **The Bible shows us the way to trust.** (Eureka!) **You can trust me that this mixture will turn into something wonderfully fun to play with if you keep stirring.** Sometimes when scary things happen to us, it seems as though good things will never happen. But the Bible shows us how to keep trusting, just as we have to keep stirring. (Children may need help stirring.)

4. After about five minutes (or when the glue becomes a solid lump in the cup), take the "Jungle Gel" out, and put it on a paper towel to absorb any remaining starch. Then let preschoolers knead it with their fingers, enjoying the rubbery, stretchy texture.

5. Put the Jungle Gel into the Gel Cells, and let children use the stickers from the "Day 1" section of their sticker sheets to decorate the cells. Thread lengths of Mini Jungle Vine through the cell loops, and tie the necklaces loosely around the children's necks. (Or if children's name badges are hung on Mini Jungle Vines, slip the Gel Cells onto the same vines!)

A CLUE FOR YOU!

Be sure to use your thumb or finger to push all the gel glue and starch out of the spoon. It's important to have even, equal measurements.

A CLUE FOR YOU!

Try this craft ahead of time so you can help children recognize what the finished product should look like. Also, if the gel doesn't quite have the correct consistency, allow it to "rest" in the Gel Cell, untouched. It works!

▼▼ Option 4: PETER'S WATER-WALK THEATER ▼▼

1. Give each child the "Treasure Land Activity Page: Day 1" activity page from his or her Preschool Student Book.

2. Carefully cut on the line. Write each child's name on his or her paper.

3. Let each child place the Jesus sticker (from the sticker sheet) at one end of the slit.

4. Put a dime-sized dollop of blue finger paint in the sea area and have each child spread it around to look like waves. Allow children to wash or wipe their hands; then draw a face on each child's index finger to be Peter.

5. Have children tell you the Bible story as they put their Peter finger puppet in the slit and "walk" across the water to Jesus. Say: ✸ **The Bible shows us the way to trust** (Eureka!), **as Peter did.**

6. Set the activity pages aside to dry.

After about seventeen minutes, blow your bamboo whistle once and announce that it's time for children to clean up their Rain Forest Exploration Stations and get ready to do some more fun things.

When cleanup is complete, blow two short blasts on the bamboo whistle. Wait for children to gather with their Clue Crews, and then say: **Now we get to go see a video. You'll be meeting a new friend named Chadder. He's a chipmunk, who has lots of crazy adventures. Hold on to your friends' hands and we'll travel together to Chadder's Treasure Hunt Theater.**

Chadder's Treasure Hunt Theater

(up to 15 minutes)

Lead children to Chadder's Treasure Hunt Theater. The Chadder's Treasure Hunt Theater Leader will greet you there and show children today's portion of *Chadder's Treasure Hunt Adventure* video. While the preschoolers are watching the video, older children will be enjoying the goodies preschoolers prepared earlier.

After the video segment, say: **Wow! Chadder is really having an adventure! He'll have to trust God to help him out of that mess!** Open a Preschool Student Book to pages 2-3. Point to the picture of Peter walking on water. Say: **In our Bible story, Peter stepped out in faith—he trusted that Jesus would care for him. Let's use our special Treasure Hunt stickers to mark this page.** Hold up a footprint sticker from a sticker sheet. **Put this footprint sticker on the page with the story of Peter. Then whenever you look at your Bible book, you can remember that this story teaches us that ✿ the Bible shows us the way to trust, just as Peter did when he walked on water!**

✿ **BIBLE POINT**

Have Clue Crew Leaders help children locate the correct page and stickers. When children have finished placing the stickers in their books, have them put their books back in the crew treasure bags. Say: **Let's hold hands and go back to our room to enjoy our special Adventure Cakes to remind us that ✿ the Bible shows us the way to trust.** (Eureka!)

✿ **BIBLE POINT**

Treasure Treats

(up to 15 minutes)

Return to your room, and have children sit at tables or in another eating area. Point out that even though Peter was frightened when he took his eyes off Jesus, Jesus did a huge miracle when Peter trusted him. Then give each child a napkin, an Adventure Cake, and a cup half-filled with water. Keep a supply of paper towels handy to wipe up any spills.

As children enjoy the snack, have Clue Crew Leaders talk with the preschoolers to get to know them better. If children finish their snacks quickly, allow them to decorate the first page of their Student Books.

When children finish their snacks, have them throw away their napkins and

cups. Then blow two short blasts on the bamboo whistle, and have children assemble in their Clue Crews.

Jungle Gym Playtime Activities
(up to 20 minutes)

If you choose to go outdoors for playtime, you may want to intersperse unstructured play with some or all of the following activities. If you remain indoors, let children revisit their favorite Rain Forest Exploration Stations, or let them engage in unstructured play. (Some of the following activities may also be appropriate for your indoor area. Use your discretion when choosing safe activities for indoor Jungle Gym Playtime Activities.)

Option 1: Hand-to-Hand Relay

Have each Clue Crew form a relay line. Determine a finish line, and have the leaders or assistant leaders stand on the finish line directly across from their crews. Each leader will walk down to his or her crew and take the hand of the first child in line. The child will walk to the finish line with eyes closed, trusting the leader to guide him or her to the finish line. Then the first child will walk back to get the second child and guide the second child to the finish. Play continues until the whole team is at the finish line.

While children are "traveling," have the whole group sing the following song to the tune of London Bridge.

> **I will trust and walk with him,**
> **Walk with him, walk with him.**
> **I will trust and walk with him.**
> **Trust in Jesus!**

Option 2: Rain Forest Ramp Run

Before class, set up a ramp on a grassy or carpeted area by placing three cinder blocks side by side. Place one end of each two-by-four on each cinder block. Lay the sheet of Masonite over the setup.

Have one leader stand on each side of the ramp. Place one-foot squares of wax paper as "rain forest leaves" at the top of the ramp. Each leader will hold a hand of the first child and help the child place each foot on a wax paper square. Tell the child to keep his or her feet together. Leaders will count to three and simultaneously pull the child rapidly down the ramp and into the grass or carpet. The child may continue to slide for a couple of feet. *Do not let go of the child's hands until he or she has stopped sliding.*

This activity requires children to completely trust the leaders, so you'll want to encourage them with the Point: � **The Bible shows us the way to trust.** (Eureka!) **We practice trust by trusting each other!** Children will want to do it again and again.

✸ **BIBLE POINT**

Option 3: Riverboat Rides

Before class, inflate the inner tubes. Use duct tape to tape down the air nozzle so it won't scratch children. Set out an inflated inner tube for each crew. Demonstrate how to sit in the tube with your shoulders and legs relaxing over the sides. Have children take turns. Let one child in each crew be the Riverboat Rider and the rest of the crew push the tube around the play area. If children are having a tough time getting the tube going, crews may wish to tie their ropes around the tube and have one child or leader pull while the rest push.

Add a dramatic flair to this activity by having a leader be a crocodile in the river while children protect their passenger by keeping him or her away from the crocodile.

Reinforce the Point: ✸ The Bible shows us the way to trust. Explain that God gives us many people to help and protect us, just as we are helping and protecting each other in the Riverboat Ride.

✸ **BIBLE POINT**

Option 4: Free Play

If you're outdoors, let children play with outdoor toys such as balls or soap bubbles or use chalk on the sidewalk. Children would also enjoy outdoor playground equipment if it's available. You can remove the Masonite from the Rain Forest Ramp Run and lay it flat on the ground. Let preschoolers take turns standing on it as Clue Crew Leaders gently move it from side to side while the child tries to stay on his or her feet. If you're indoors, let children play with classroom toys such as blocks, stuffed animals, or modeling dough. (Check out the recipe for our Delightful Dough on page 34. Children will love the sweet scent!) As children play, look for opportunities to review today's Point and Bible story.

After about fifteen minutes, blow the bamboo whistle once to let children know it's time to finish their activities and clean up. If you're outside, blow the bamboo whistle twice after cleanup is complete to signal your return to the classroom. Then gather in the story area for singing.

Delightful Dough

Mix together:

1 cup flour
1 cup water
2 teaspoons cream of tartar
½ cup salt
1 tablespoon vegetable oil
1 package of unsweetened powdered drink mix (any flavor)

Cook the mixture over medium heat in a saucepan, stirring constantly until the mixture pulls away from the sides of the pan. Place the dough on wax paper and knead it until it is smooth. Store in resealable plastic bags or containers.

A CLUE FOR YOU!

At the field test, we decorated a small trunk with equipment used by explorers, such as a compass, a map, and small garden tools. We had a gold pouch that held our special treasure each day. The children loved it!

— — — — — — — —

Sing-Along Surprise

(up to 15 minutes)

Before class, determine something that can be used as a treasure box. It can be an old jewelry box, a file box spray-painted gold, or a cardboard box tied shut with twine. Be as simple or elaborate as you wish. You can fill the box with fun-looking treasures or leave it empty except for the surprise of the day.

The surprise for today is a Bible. Say: **Each day at Sing-Along Surprise, one of the things we have used during the day will be our secret treasure. I'll tell you a riddle, and you see if you can guess what the secret treasure is. Here's the riddle for today:**

I'm a book.
I'm God's own Word.
I'm filled with stories
Many have heard.

Let children guess, then reveal your secret treasure. Tell children why the Bible is a treasure to you!

Say: **Let's sing some songs together to remind us that ✪ the Bible shows us the way to trust.** (Eureka!)

Lead children in singing one or more of the following songs.

✪ BIBLE POINT

I Will Trust and Walk With Him

(Sing to the tune of "London Bridge.")

Have children stand up and hold hands to form a circle. As they sing, have them walk around clockwise.

**I will trust and walk with him,
Walk with him, walk with him.
I will trust and walk with him,
Trust in Jesus!**

Trust, Trust in Jesus

(Sing to the tune of "Jesus Loves Me.")

**I can trust him, this I know
For my Bible tells me so.
When I work and when I play,
I can trust him every day.**

**Trust, trust in Jesus.
Trust, trust in Jesus.
Trust, trust in Jesus.
Yes, I can trust him.**

Using the *Preschool Bible Treasure Land* audiocassette, lead children in singing "The B-I-B-L-E."

A CLUE FOR YOU!

Use the counter on your cassette player to cue the songs from the *Preschool Bible Treasure Land* audio-cassette.

The B–I–B–L–E

(March in place.)

The B! *(First section pumps fists overhead.)*
The I! *(Second section pumps fists overhead.)*
The B! *(Third section pumps fists overhead.)*
L-E! *(Everybody pumps fists overhead.)*

The B! *(First section pumps fists overhead.)*
The I! *(Second section pumps fists overhead.)*
The B! *(Third section pumps fists overhead.)*
L-E! *(Everybody pumps fists overhead.)*

The B-I-B-L-E *(move hands from right, to center, to left, to center),*
Yes, that's the book for me. *(Move hands from right, to center, to left, to center.)*
I stand alone on the Word of God *(move hands from right, to center, to left, to center),*
The B-I-B-L-E! *(Move hands from right, to center, to left, to center.)*

The B-I-B-L-E *(move hands from right, to center, to left, to center),*
Yes, that's the book for me. *(Move hands from right, to center, to left, to center.)*
I stand alone on the Word of God *(move hands from right, to center, to left, to center),*
The B-I-B-L-E! *(Move hands from right, to center, to left, to center.)*

Leader: **The B!** *(Leader cups hands around mouth.)*
Section 1: **The B!** *(First section pumps fists overhead.)*
Leader: **The I!** *(Leader cups hands around mouth.)*
Section 2: **The I!** *(Second section pumps fists overhead.)*
Leader: **The B!** *(Leader cups hands around mouth.)*
Section 3: **The B!** *(Third section pumps fists overhead.)*
Everyone: **L-E!** *(Everybody pumps fists overhead.)*

Leader: **The B!** *(Leader cups hands around mouth.)*
Section 1: **The B!** *(First section pumps fists overhead.)*
Leader: **The I!** *(Leader cups hands around mouth.)*
Section 2: **The I!** *(Second section pumps fists overhead.)*
Leader: **The B!** *(Leader cups hands around mouth.)*
Section 3: **The B!** *(Third section pumps fists overhead.)*
Everyone: **L-E!** *(Everybody pumps fists overhead.)*

The B-I-B-L-E *(move hands from right, to center, to left, to center),*
Yes, that's the book for me. *(Move hands from right, to center, to left, to center.)*
I stand alone on the Word of God *(move hands from right, to center, to left, to center),*
The B-I-B-L-E! *(Move hands from right, to center, to left, to center.)*

The B-I-B-L-E *(move hands from right, to center, to left, to center),*
Yes, that's the book for me. *(Move hands from right, to center, to left, to center.)*
I stand alone on the Word of God *(move hands from right, to center, to left, to center),*
I stand alone on the Word of God *(march in place),*
I stand alone on the Word of God *(march in place),*
The B-I-B-L-E! *(Punch fists out and up gradually, ending with palms open.)*

✸ **BIBLE POINT**

Say: **I've seen a lot of trust in our Preschool Bible Treasure Land today. I can tell that you are learning ✸ the Bible shows us the way to trust.** (Eureka!)

Choose one crew at a time to stand and be affirmed. Have children shout out a cheer for each crew. For example, if one crew is named Monkeys, have them stand while the whole group shouts:

**"Monkeys, Monkeys,
One, two, three.
They trust Jesus.**

Way to be!"

After each crew has been affirmed and is seated, ask:

● **What was your favorite activity today?** (Planting seeds; sliding down the ramp.)

● **What was the hardest activity for you today?** (Water-walking; making snacks.)

● **Who helped you with the hardest activity?** (My friend; you; my crew leader.)

Say: **God gives us lots of helpers who help us learn to trust and** ✪ **the Bible shows us the way to trust!** (Eureka!) **Jesus helped Peter learn about trust in our Bible story today. Let's sing a song about Peter!**

Have children pretend to get into a boat and sway back and forth as they sing this song to the tune of "My Bonnie Lies Over the Ocean."

The wind blew the boat on the water.
The wind blew the boat on the sea.
Then Jesus walked out on the water,
And Peter was brave as could be!
He said (Leader says...),
"Jesus, Jesus, I want to come out there to you, to you."
Jesus said (Leader says...),
"Peter, Peter, I want you to come out here, too!"

So Peter walked out on the water.
So Peter walked out on the sea.
The wind kept on blowing the water.
And Peter was scared as could be.
He said:
"Save me, oh, save me! I'm scared that I'm going to drown, to drown.
Jesus said:
"Reach out your hand to me! I promise I won't let you down!

Well, Peter, he learned a great lesson
Out on the stormy sea.
Peter, he learned to trust Jesus,
And his story helps me to see:
I can trust, yes, I can trust Jesus, my friend, my friend!
I can trust, yes, I can trust Jesus, my friend!

(Song adapted from *Wiggly, Giggly Bible Stories About Jesus,* Copyright ©
Group Publishing, Inc., P.O. Box 481, Loveland, CO 80539.)

✪ **BIBLE POINT**

Field Test Findings

Our Clue Crew Leaders told us that they would have appreciated having copies of the words to the songs so that they could help children review them in their spare moments or use them as travel songs along the way. You may want to photocopy the "Preschool Songs" on page 40 of this leader manual so your crew leaders can use them!

Using the *Preschool Bible Treasure Land* audiocassette, lead children in singing "I've Found Me a Treasure, Day 1."

I've Found Me a Treasure (Day 1)

Chorus:

I've found me a treasure (*put hands next to mouth as if shouting and bounce from right to left with the beat*);
I've found a friend. (*Keep hands next to mouth and bounce from left to right.*)
I found Jesus (*sign "Jesus"*),
And his love will never end. (*Cross arms over chest on "love," extend right arm to side on "never," and extend left arm to side on "end."*)
I've found me a treasure (*put hands next to mouth as if shouting and bounce from right to left with the beat*);
I've found a friend. (*Keep hands next to mouth and bounce from left to right.*)
I found Jesus (*sign "Jesus"*),
And his love will never end. (*Cross arms over chest on "love," extend right arm to side on "never," and extend left arm to side on "end."*)

Day 1:

Jesus came upon a boat (*sign "Jesus"*)
While walking on the sea. (*Walk in place.*)
Peter trusted in his Lord (*raise arms overhead*)
And stepped out on the Galilee. (*Walk in place.*)

(Repeat chorus)

After the last song, blow two short blasts on the bamboo whistle and have children assemble in their Clue Crews for Treasure Time Finale. Be sure children are holding hands or the crew ropes as they travel.

Treasure Time Finale
(up to 20 minutes)

Lead children to the room you're using for Treasure Time Finale. The Treasure Time Finale Leader will greet you and show you where to sit.

Preschoolers and older kids will sing songs and then see an amazing experiment with a balloon. Children will then use balloons to celebrate the fact that they can trust Jesus.

When the Treasure Time Finale Leader dismisses everyone, have preschoolers remain seated with their Clue Crew Leaders in the Treasure Time Finale area until their parents or caregivers arrive to pick them up. While children are waiting,

A CLUE FOR YOU!

If you've set the "Peter's Water-Walk Theater" pictures aside to dry, have Clue Crew Leaders retrieve them before leading children to Treasure Time Finale.

A CLUE FOR YOU!

Depending on your VBS format, you may want to leave the Mini Rain Forests in your Preschool Bible Treasure Land area all week. Children will love watching the seeds sprout and grow; plus, you'll add authentic rain forest decor to your room!

have Clue Crew Leaders collect their crew members' name badges and place them in their crew treasure bags.

Remind children to take their Rain Forest Exploration Station projects with them when they leave. Be sure to thank parents and caregivers for bringing their children to Treasure Hunt Bible Adventure.

A CLUE FOR YOU!

It's important to remind Clue Crew Leaders to never let their crew members out of sight until children are retrieved by parents.

39

PRESCHOOL SONGS

I Will Trust and Walk With Him

(Sing to the tune of "London Bridge.")

I will trust and walk with him,
Walk with him, walk with him.
I will trust and walk with him,
Trust in Jesus!

Trust, Trust in Jesus

(Sing to the tune of "Jesus Loves Me.")

I can trust him, this I know
For my Bible tells me so.
When I work and when I play,
I can trust him every day.

Trust, trust in Jesus.
Trust, trust in Jesus.
Trust, trust in Jesus.
Yes, I can trust him.

The Bible Shows Us the Way to Live

(Sing to the tune of "Here We Go 'Round the Mulberry Bush.")

The Bible shows us the way to live,
Way to live, way to live.
The Bible shows us the way to live
As children of God.

BIBLE POINT

The Bible shows us the way to love.

BIBLE BASIS

John 13:1-17. Jesus washes the disciples' feet.

Jesus knew that his time on earth was coming to an end. His purpose would soon be accomplished, and he could return to heaven, to the side of the Father. Jesus' time with the disciples was coming to an end too. These followers, who gave up everything to follow Jesus and learn from him, must now carry his message to the world. What parting words would Jesus leave with them? How could he express his love for them and prepare them for the challenges ahead? Jesus' words were almost unnecessary, for his actions were unforgettable. The Son of God lowered himself to the position of a servant and washed his disciples' dusty feet. In this one simple act, Jesus demonstrated the depth of his love and modeled the servant's heart he desired in his followers.

It goes against human nature to put the needs of others ahead of our own. Our culture says to "look out for number one." We read magazines with titles such as Self and Moi. And we eat at restaurants where we can have it our way. Our world sends a self-centered and egocentric message to children, as well. That's why the children at your VBS can learn so much from Jesus' demonstration of love and humility. In today's activities, kids will experience the power of loving others through selfless acts. Children will discover that Jesus' actions are as unforgettable today as they were for the disciples nearly two thousand years ago.

▼ TREASURE LAND SCHEDULE ▼

LOCATION	ACTIVITY	MINUTES	WHAT CHILDREN WILL DO	CLASSROOM SUPPLIES	PRESCHOOL STUDENT BOOK SUPPLIES
	Treasure Hunt Sing & Play	up to 20	Sing Treasure Hunt Bible Adventure songs with older children.	Name badges	
Preschool Bible Treasure Land	Report for Adventure!	up to 10	Meet their classmates and get into their Clue Crews.	Name badges, "Bible Point" posters	
Preschool Bible Treasure Land	Bible Story Search Party	up to 15	Take a story treasure hunt to find out how Jesus showed his friends the way to love.	"Passover Treasure Hunt" photocopies (p. 46), three bedsheets or Bible-time costumes, baby wipes, a bath towel, scented baby lotion, Crock-Pot of spices (optional)	
Preschool Bible Treasure Land	Rain Forest Exploration Stations	up to 25	**Option 1: Housekeeping Center**—Set the table for a big dinner.	Toy housekeeping items	Treasure Land Activity Page: Day 2
			Option 2: Love Towels—Print hearts on washcloths to help remember that Jesus washed his friends' feet.	Blocks, plastic wrap, craft glue, craft foam hearts, sponge paintbrushes, red fabric paint, white washcloths	
			Option 3: Surprise Treasure Chests—Make treasure chests to keep wonderful surprises in.	Surprise Treasure Chest Kits, markers, Treasure Hunt sticker sheets	
			Option 4: Clean Feet—Glue Bubble Wrap bubbles on the Bible picture of Jesus washing his disciples' feet.	Bubble Wrap scraps, glue, crayons, scissors	
	Chadder's Treasure Hunt Theater	up to 15	Hear how Chadder Chipmunk learns about loving others, mark the Bible story with a heart sticker, and learn about Operation Kid-to-Kid.	Treasure Hunt sticker sheets	Preschool Student Books (pp. 4-5), Spanish Gospels of John
Preschool Bible Treasure Land	Treasure Treats	up to 15	Enjoy Love Chests and tell leaders about the people they love.	Snacks provided by the Treasure Treats Leader	
	Jungle Gym Playtime Activities	up to 20	**Option 1: Foot-Washing Relay**—Dry each other's feet in this active game.	Wading pool, water, paper towels	
			Option 2: Hug Tag—Play a simple Tag game and "unfreeze" friends with hugs.		
			Option 3: Foot Fishing—Try to remove items from a pool using only their feet.	Small toys, wading pool filled with water	
			Option 4: Free Play—Enjoy free play outdoors or in the classroom.	Playground equipment, classroom toys, bubble solution, bucket, wire coat hangers, masking tape	
Preschool Bible Treasure Land	Sing-Along Surprise	up to 15	Sing Bible action songs.	Treasure box; Surprise Treasure Chests; Treasure Hunt sticker sheets; cassette player; *Preschool Bible Treasure Land* audiocassette: "Children, Children"; "Jesus Loves Me"; "I've Found Me a Treasure"	
	Treasure Time Finale	up to 20	Sing songs and see how someone shows love to the Treasure Time Finale Leader.		

Preschool Bible Treasure Land Prep

Before children arrive:

● Set up an Upper Room (see Mark 14:15) where you'll tell the Bible story. If you want to add to your "scent-sational" drama, have a Crock-Pot of spices simmering in the room. Set baby wipes near the door.

● Choose three doors near your Preschool Bible Treasure Land area that children can easily find. You'll send three volunteers in costume to the rooms to give children clues during Bible Story Search Party.

● Post "Bible Point" posters where children can easily see them.

● Choose which Rain Forest Exploration Stations you'll use, and collect the supplies you'll need. If children will be making Love Towels, prepare the blocks for printing by wrapping plastic wrap around each block and then gluing a craft foam heart to it. This will look like a rubber stamp.

● Choose which Jungle Gym Playtime Activities you'll use, and collect the supplies you'll need.

● Choose which Sing-Along Surprise songs you'll use, and cue the *Preschool Bible Treasure Land* audiocassette to the first song you've chosen.

● Consult with the Treasure Treats Leader to find out what time the Treasure Treats Service Crew will deliver your snacks.

Treasure Hunt Sing & Play
(up to 20 minutes)

Before children arrive, arrange with the Treasure Hunt Sing & Play Leader to reserve seats up front for your preschoolers.

Greet children as they arrive. Clue Crew Leaders can give children their name badges and then sit with children and involve them in this sing-along time. Preschoolers will enjoy hearing the music and doing the motions right along with the big kids!

After the Treasure Hunt Director dismisses your group, have children hold hands in their Clue Crews. Travel together to your Preschool Bible Treasure Land room.

Report for Adventure!
(up to 10 minutes)

After you arrive in your room, make sure each child is wearing his or her name badge.

You can expect new children to visit Treasure Hunt Bible Adventure each day, so be prepared with extra name badges. Assign new children to Clue Crews that have fewer than five children in them. If most of your crews are full, check with your Treasure Hunt Director to see if he or she has recruited any extra volunteers you might use as Clue Crew Leaders.

Field Test Findings

Preschool crafts and elementary crafts are not the same! Today preschoolers make Surprise Treasure Chests—the same craft elementary kids make on Day 3. We discovered that preschoolers easily connected the "love" theme with the treasure chests—which "sing" the song "Jesus Loves Me."

A CLUE FOR YOU!

Post a sign on your Preschool Bible Treasure Land door to let parents know you're meeting in the Treasure Hunt Sing & Play area.

— **EXTRA IDEA!** —

For added fun, have a Chadder Chipmunk puppet blow the bamboo whistle (with your help, of course!) and review with children the procedure to form Clue Crews. Your preschoolers will love seeing Chadder Chipmunk in their classroom!

⊛ **BIBLE POINT**

⊛ **BIBLE POINT**

Blow your bamboo whistle once. Say: **Welcome to Treasure Hunt Bible Adventure! Remember my bamboo whistle? When I blow the bamboo whistle once, it means I want you to look at me.**

Blow the bamboo whistle twice. Ask:

● **Who remembers what two short whistle blasts mean?**

Let children respond. If most of the children were in Treasure Hunt Bible Adventure yesterday, they'll probably remember and may even assemble in their Clue Crews without further instructions.

Say: **When I blow the bamboo whistle two short times, I want you to quickly gather with your Clue Crew. Let's practice that.** Help children practice finding their crews as you blow the bamboo whistle two short times. Help new children find their assigned crews. Lead crews to the wall where you've posted the "Bible Point" posters.

Ask:

● **Yesterday we learned** ⊛ **the Bible shows us the way to trust.** (Eureka!)

Say: **Our Bible story showed us how Peter trusted Jesus as the two of them walked on the water together. Today we're learning that** ⊛ **the Bible shows us the way to love.** (Eureka!) **Whenever you hear me say, "The Bible shows us the way to love," remember to shout "Eureka!" Remember, "Eureka" means "I found something special!"**

Our Bible story is about an incredible way Jesus showed his friends the way to love. We're going on a treasure hunt during our Bible story today! You'll hear parts of the story in several different places. To make sure you know who everyone in your crew is, let's have each Clue Crew stand together in a different area of the room. Move to your area just as the animal your crew is named after would move, and then we'll learn our new crew cheer for the day.

Have each crew move together to a specified area of the room. Then stand in the center and teach them this cheer:

[Crew name, crew name],

One, two, three.

We love like Jesus.

Way to be!

Have each crew leader discuss with his or her crew ways they can show love. Then ask for a report from each group.

Say: **I'm going to go and get ready for our Bible story. In a minute or two, your Clue Crew Leaders will take you on a treasure hunt! You'll be looking for a room where a big dinner is. To find the big dinner, you'll knock on three different doors. When someone opens the door, tell them, "We're looking for a room where there's a big dinner." You'll need to listen carefully and follow the clues to find our Bible story room.**

Instruct Clue Crew Leaders how to lead children through the Bible Story Search Party. If you have more than twenty preschoolers, we recommend that Clue Crews go on this treasure hunt at one-minute intervals. As children wait with their Clue Crews, leaders can direct children in singing, discussing yesterday's Bible story, or simply getting to know each other. (Remember, it's *only* one minute!)

Let Clue Crew Leaders lead children to each of the three clue givers, then to knock on the door where you will tell the story. This process will allow more children to interact with your "actors" and will allow you to wash each child's feet, without others waiting in line. Gather all Clue Crews in your Upper Room before beginning the Bible story.

A CLUE FOR YOU!

It's important to tell Clue Crew Leaders where the Upper Room is set up. They'll guide children to find the room, where you'll tell the Bible story.

PASSOVER TREASURE HUNT

Clue 1

You're a grumpy village citizen who's under a lot of pressure to get ready for Passover. When children knock at your door, answer it somewhat gruffly.

Say: **No, no, I don't know where your Passover meal is to be served. Jesus' friends were in town a few days ago, but they didn't mention anything about their holiday plans. Go ask my neighbor. I think they borrowed a donkey colt from him.**

Clue 2

You're kind and gentle and really want to help children find their destination.

Say: **Big dinner? Oh, you mean the Passover feast this Thursday night. Hmm...let me think. They borrowed my donkey—said the Lord needed it. I really thought they'd have brought the dear little thing back by now. Didn't really say where they were going, but I got the impression they might head for Jerusalem. So you've been invited to dinner, but you don't know where you're going. Hmm...check with my friend the baker in Jerusalem. He bakes bread for everyone. He may have seen them. I really hope you find the place before sundown. Hurry along, now. Remember...the baker's.**

Clue 3

You're the baker in Jerusalem. You know everyone and everything about life in the city.

Say: **Jesus' Passover feast? Sure, sure, I know where they're having it. They picked up their bread about an hour ago. Said they were headed for the Upper Room in the next block, right over there. Glad I can be of help to such a fine bunch of children. Shalom, peace to you and your leaders.**

Bible Story Search Party

(up to 15 minutes)

Before class, photocopy and cut apart the clues found on page 46. Adapt this story plan to fit your situation. You can have three different helpers behind three doors and use a sign on each door that corresponds to the clue: "Clue 1," Clue 2," or "Clue 3." Or you can use one person who remains behind the same door, dressed in different costumes. If you follow this plan, have preschoolers take an imaginary walk between each knock. Give the clues to your volunteer(s). Make sure the children hear the clues in the correct order!

Wrap a towel around your waist, and wait in the Upper Room until children arrive.

When children knock at your door, greet each one warmly.

Say: **Welcome! I'm so glad you found your way to the big dinner room. I'm going to wipe your shoes before you come in. Jesus washed his friends' feet the night of the big dinner to show them how much he loved them. ✸ The Bible shows us the way to love** (Eureka!) **in the same way Jesus showed his friends the way to love.**

Continue to repeat the Point as you wipe each child's shoes with a baby wipe. Dry them with the towel around your waist. Have children be seated as soon as you are done wiping their shoes. When all the children have arrived and are seated, ask:

● **Who has washed your feet before?** (My mom; my dad; no one.)

● **Why do you think that person was willing to wash your dirty feet?** (He loves me; she didn't want me to get the floor dirty.)

Say: **In Bible times, people wore sandals and their feet got very dusty and dirty. It was the job of a servant to wash the bare feet of dinner guests. But Jesus wanted to serve his friends by washing their feet. He tied a towel around his waist and knelt down to wipe away all the dirt. It was a loving, kind thing for Jesus to do. Today we don't wash our guests feet, but we can help each other in other ways.** Ask:

● **What are some ways you can help others?** (By giving them a drink of water; by helping my mom take care of my baby sister.)

● **What are some ways you can make people feel good?** (By telling them nice things; by rubbing my mom's back; by smiling.)

Say: **We're going to serve each other right now by rubbing some nice-smelling lotion onto each other's hands to make the other person feel good.**

Pour some lotion into the Clue Crew Leaders' hands, and let them distribute it to their groups. When the groups are finished, say: **Now smell your hands. As you smell that nice clean smell today, remember that Jesus served his friends to show his love, just as you served each other. ✸ The Bible shows us the way to love** (Eureka!) **just as Jesus did.**

Before we go to our Rain Forest Exploration Stations, I'd like each crew to huddle in a "love hug" and say your crew cheer together!

✸ **BIBLE POINT**

Field Test Findings

Due to a little confusion on the part of our volunteers, some children heard the clues out of order. Even so, all the children had their "feet" washed in a kind, loving manner. That was the most important part anyway!

✸ **BIBLE POINT**

RAIN FOREST EXPLORATION STATIONS

(up to 25 minutes)

▼▼ Option 1: HOUSEKEEPING CENTER ▼▼▼▼▼▼▼

1. As children play with housekeeping items, encourage them to set the table as though they're preparing for a big dinner.

2. Ask children how they can show love while they're preparing for the dinner.

3. Say: ✽ **The Bible shows us the way to love.** (Eureka!) **We can love others by helping them the way Jesus helped his friends.**

▼▼ Option 2: LOVE TOWELS ▼▼▼▼▼▼▼▼▼▼▼▼

1. Hand each child a white washcloth. Make sure it's marked with his or her name.

2. Help each child brush a coat of red paint over the heart only, with a paintbrush. (You may wish to clean off any paint that's on the block before the child prints with it.)

3. Let children place the blocks heart-side down on the washcloths and press.

4. Repeat the process until the child has stamped as many hearts as desired.

5. Tell children they can take these towels home to serve others in their families. Ask them how they might be able to use them. Children may answer that they can wash tables or wipe a little brother's face. Say: ✽ **The Bible shows us the way to love.** (Eureka!) **I can see you're already planning ways to show your family God's love.**

6. Let the paint on the towels dry before folding them.

RAIN FOREST EXPLORATION STATIONS

▼▼ Option 3: SURPRISE TREASURE CHESTS ▼▼▼▼▼

1. Show children a finished Surprise Treasure Chest so they will know what theirs will look like.

2. Let children color their treasure chests with markers.

3. Help children fold the boxes; then let them add the stickers from the "Day 2" section of the sticker sheets.

While children are decorating their treasure chests, affix a Singing Surprise sticker so that it fits exactly inside the rectangle inside each chest. Say: ✿ **The Bible shows us the way to love.** (Eureka!) **Every act of love you do is a treasure to someone.**

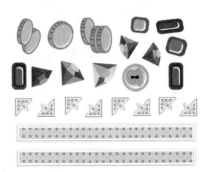

▼▼ Option 4: CLEAN FEET ▼▼▼▼▼▼▼▼▼▼▼▼▼▼

1. Give each child the "Treasure Land Activity Page: Day 2" from his or her Preschool Student Book.

2. Set out crayons, glue, scissors, and Bubble Wrap scraps. Show children how to cut individual bubbles from the bubble wrap. Let children color their pictures. Then help them glue the Bubble Wrap scraps around the basin Jesus is using in the picture so that they look like floating bubbles.

As children work, review the details of Jesus washing his friends' feet. Remind them that Jesus loved his friends by serving them. Serving is one way ✿ the Bible shows us the way to love.

A CLUE FOR YOU!

"Aren't preschoolers too young to understand about Bibles and other languages?" Not in the least! Many preschool programs teach children simple words in Spanish or other languages. This is a wonderful way to help little ones feel empowered to do big things, while teaching them that God's Word is for everyone!

After about seventeen minutes, blow your bamboo whistle once and announce that it's time for children to clean up their Rain Forest Exploration Stations and get ready to do some more fun things.

When cleanup is complete, blow two short blasts on the bamboo whistle. Wait for children to gather with their Clue Crews, and then say: **Now we get to go see a video. Do you remember our new friend Chadder Chipmunk? We met him yesterday in a crazy treasure hunt adventure. What do you remember about Chadder Chipmunk's adventure?** Children may recall that Chadder went on a treasure hunt, that Chadder met two friends, or that Chadder and his friends were in a cave.

Say: **Let's see what kind of adventure is in store for Chadder Chipmunk today as he travels through Treasure Hunt Bible Adventure! Take hold of your friends' hands. We'll travel together to Chadder's Treasure Hunt Theater.**

Chadder's Treasure Hunt Theater
(up to 15 minutes)

Lead children to Chadder's Treasure Hunt Theater. The Chadder's Treasure Hunt Theater Leader will greet you there and show children today's portion of *Chadder's Treasure Hunt Adventure* video.

After the video segment, open a Preschool Student Book and show children the Gospel of John they will be giving to a Spanish-speaking child. Talk a little about how Chadder showed love in the video. Have Clue Crew Leaders open children's Student Books to pages 4-5 that illustrate Jesus washing his friends' feet. Show children how to place the large heart sticker on the edge of the page. Ask:

● **When you want to remember the way Jesus loved, how can you find that page in your Bible right away?** (By looking for the sticker; when I see the heart sticker, I'll remember that Jesus showed love.)

Say: **Children in Spanish-speaking countries need to learn about God's love, too. We've learned the song "Jesus Loves Me" in Sing & Play. Instead of saying "Jesus loves me," children who speak Spanish would say "Jesus [Hay-soos] mi amor." Let's try to say that together: "Hay-soos me ah-more." That means "Jesus loves me!"**

Have children close their books. Clue Crew Leaders can put them into the treasure bags.

Say: **Right now it's time for us to go back to our room for snacks. Let's get into our Clue Crews and hold hands as we travel.**

Treasure Treats

(up to 15 minutes)

Return to your room, and have children sit down at tables or in another eating area. Point out that today's snack looks like a little treasure chest with a heart in it. Give each child a napkin, a Love Chest, and a cup half-filled with juice. Keep a supply of paper towels handy to wipe up any spills.

Say: **Jesus showed his love to the people he lived with and worked with. The Bible shows us the way to love all the people we live with and work with, too.** (Eureka!) **As you're eating your snack today, tell your crew leader about the people you love!**

Before we have our snack, we're going to thank God for each person here in a special way. I'm going to say each letter of the alphabet. When I say the first letter of your name, I want you to pop up and say your name. Let's try a few letters so you can practice: C (pause), **J** (pause), **R** (pause).

That's great! After everyone has popped up, the rest of us will thank God for a loving friend like you. Let's practice by having everyone with an "R" name stand back up again.

Wait for all the R-named children to stand up, and then lead the rest of the class in saying, "Thank you, God, for [name of child]." Point to each child before you pray for him or her. If you don't have any R names in your class, practice with a different letter.

After you've practiced, have the R-named children sit down, and then go through the alphabet. Each time children pop up, lead the rest of the class in thanking God for them.

After all the children have popped up, say: **All of this popping up and down is making me hungry. Let's thank God for these yummy snacks so we can eat them up!**

Invite a child to thank God for the snack and then let children dig in! As children enjoy the snack, have Clue Crew Leaders ask children questions about the people they love.

When children finish their snacks, have them throw away their napkins and cups. Then blow two short blasts on the bamboo whistle and have children assemble in their Clue Crews.

BIBLE POINT

A CLUE FOR YOU!

If you have a Chadder Chipmunk puppet, have him pop up and call out "Thank you, God, for Chadder Chipmunk!" when you call out the letters A, B, and C. When he pops up for A and B, have children help you instruct Chadder Chipmunk that his name starts with C, and he'll have to wait until you call the letter C.

A CLUE FOR YOU!

Most of the children in your class probably know their alphabet. If some children don't stand up when their letters are called, gently encourage them. For example, you can say, "Ian, your name starts with the letter I. It's your turn to stand up now!"

Jungle Gym Playtime Activities
(up to 20 minutes)

If you choose to go outdoors for playtime, you may want to intersperse unstructured play with some or all of the following activities. If you remain indoors, let children revisit their favorite Rain Forest Exploration Stations or let them engage in unstructured play. (Some of the following activities may also be appropriate for your indoor area. Use your discretion when choosing safe activities for indoor Jungle Gym Playtime Activities.)

Option 1: Foot-Washing Relay

Have each Clue Crew form a relay line a short distance from the wading pool and remove their shoes. The crew leader will stand by the pool and call a crew member's name. The child will run to the wading pool and step in, then the Clue Crew Leader will dry that child's feet with a paper towel. The child may then call the next person to come and have his or her feet washed. Continue until all the children have had their feet washed.

Option 2: Hug Tag

Play this game in a confined area. Choose one person to be "It." Ask the child to try to tag other children. If a child is tagged, he or she must "freeze" until another child comes along and hugs him or her. You may wish to pick a Clue Crew Leader as "It" to start the game.

Option 3: Foot Fishing

Fill a wading pool with a variety of small toys. Have crew members remove their shoes and then try to fish the toys out of the pool, using only their feet! When one crew has successfully emptied the pool, have them replace the toys for the next crew.

Option 4: Free Play

Consider making up a bucket of bubble solution with one cup of Joy dishwashing liquid, one tablespoon of glycerin, and one gallon of water. (Ask the Treasure Hunt Director if he or she has purchased these supplies.) Make big heart-shaped bubble blowers by straightening wire clothes hangers and shaping them into hearts with a handle. Put masking tape around any rough edges.

If you're outdoors, let children play with outdoor toys such as balls or soap bubbles or use chalk on the sidewalk. Children would also enjoy outdoor playground equipment if it's available. If you're indoors, let children play with classroom toys such as blocks, stuffed animals, or modeling dough. As children play, look for opportunities to review today's Point and Bible story.

After about fifteen minutes, blow the bamboo whistle once to let children know it's time to finish their activities and clean up. If you're outside, blow the bamboo whistle twice after cleanup is complete to signal your return to the classroom. Then gather in the story area for singing.

A CLUE FOR YOU!

Be sure children don't jump into the pool. The bottom of the pool may be slick and children could slip and fall.

Sing-Along Surprise

(up to 15 minutes)

The surprise for today is the giant heart sticker from the Treasure Hunt sticker sheet. You'll need one for your treasure box. The Clue Crew Leaders will have the smaller heart stickers to help the children put them into their Surprise Treasure Chests.

Say: **It's time to share the secret treasure with you. It's hidden right here in my secret treasure box. Here's the riddle for today:**

Nothing can ever keep us apart.

God's love is always

Here in my... (Let children complete the riddle with the word "heart.")

Reveal your secret treasure. Then have crew leaders help each child place a small heart sticker on the inside of his or her Surprise Treasure Chest.

Say: **God's love is a special treasure to remember always. God loved us so much that he sent his Son, Jesus, and gave us ✤ the Bible to show us the way to love!** (Eureka!)

Say: **Let's sing some songs together to remind us that ✤ the Bible shows us the way to love.** (Eureka!)

Lead children in singing one or more of the following songs.

✤ **BIBLE POINT**

✤ **BIBLE POINT**

Children, Children

Children, children , come and listen,
Come and hear of Jesus' love.
Children, children, come and see him,
Come and see how Jesus loves.
Children, children, come and touch him,
Come and touch our Bible friend.
Jesus, Jesus, come and bless us,
Come and bless us with your love.

"Children, Children" by Robert C. Evans. Copyright © 1982 Integrity's Hosanna! Music/ASCAP.
All rights reserved. International copyright secured. Used by permission.

Say: ✤ **The Bible shows us the way to love!** (Eureka!) Ask:

● **How did our Bible story today show us the way to love?** (Jesus was loving to his friends; Jesus did something nice for his friends.)

● **How have you seen others being loving today?** (My leader hugged me; someone gave his drink to his crew leader.)

Say: **Let's do our group cheer with the** [crew name]!

[Crew name, crew name],

One, two, three.

They love like Jesus.

Way to be!

✤ **BIBLE POINT**

✤ BIBLE POINT

Say: **I'm so glad ✤ the Bible shows us the way to love!** (Eureka!) **Let's sing a song that tells us more about Jesus' love!**

Jesus Loves Me

(To the beat, lean forward and back while shaking shoulders and snapping.)
Jesus loves me! This I know *(do the basic hip-hop step),*
For the Bible tells me so. *(Do the basic hip-hop step.)*
Little ones to him belong *(do the basic hip-hop step);*
They are weak, but he is strong. *(Do the basic hip-hop step.)*

Yes, Jesus loves me! *(Sign the words.)*
Yes, Jesus loves me! *(Sign the words.)*
Yes, Jesus loves me! *(Sign the words.)*
The Bible tells me so. *(Turn in a circle, shaking jazz hands overhead.)*

(To the beat, lean forward and then back while shaking shoulders and snapping.)
Jesus loves me! He will stay *(do the basic hip-hop step)*
Close beside me all the way. *(Do the basic hip-hop step.)*
If I love him, when I die *(do the basic hip-hop step),*
He will take me home on high. *(Do the basic hip-hop step.)*

Yes, Jesus loves me! *(Sign the words.)*
Yes, Jesus loves me! *(Sign the words.)*
Yes, Jesus loves me! *(Sign the words.)*
The Bible tells me so. *(Turn in a circle, shaking jazz hands overhead.)*

Jesus loves me! This I know *(do the basic hip-hop step),*
For the Bible tells me so. *(Do the basic hip-hop step.)*
Little ones to him belong *(do the basic hip-hop step);*
They are weak, but he is strong. *(Do the basic hip-hop step.)*

Yes, Jesus loves me! *(Sign the words.)*
Yes, Jesus loves me! *(Sign the words.)*
Yes, Jesus loves me! *(Sign the words.)*
The Bible tells me so. *(Turn in a circle, shaking jazz hands overhead.)*

Yes, Jesus loves me! *(Sign the words.)*
Yes, Jesus loves me! *(Sign the words.)*
Yes, Jesus loves me! *(Sign the words.)*
The Bible tells me so. *(Turn in a circle, shaking jazz hands overhead.)*
(To the beat, lean forward and then back while shaking shoulders and snapping.)

Say: **At Treasure Hunt Bible Adventure, we're learning all about the treasures in the Bible. Let's close by singing our Treasure Hunt Bible Adventure theme song!**

I've Found Me a Treasure (Day 2)

Chorus:

I've found me a treasure *(put hands next to mouth as if shouting and bounce from right to left with the beat);*
I've found a friend. *(Keep hands next to mouth and bounce from left to right.)*
I found Jesus *(sign "Jesus"),*
And his love will never end. *(Cross arms over chest on "love," extend right arm to side on "never," and extend left arm to side on "end.")*
I've found me a treasure *(put hands next to mouth as if shouting and bounce from right to left with the beat);*
I've found a friend. *(Keep hands next to mouth and bounce from left to right.)*
I found Jesus *(sign "Jesus"),*
And his love will never end. *(Cross arms over chest on "love," extend right arm to side on "never," and extend left arm to side on "end.")*

Day 2:

Jesus taught us how to love *(sign "Jesus" and then cross arms over chest)*
In hopes that we may see *(shade eyes with hands)*
No one's greater than the next. *(Hold hands up and shake them back and forth);*
Then he washed his disciples' feet. *(Slap the bottom of one foot with the opposite hand.)*

(Repeat chorus)

Have Clue Crew Leaders collect their children's Surprise Treasure Chests. Leaders will take them, along with any other Rain Forest Exploration Station projects and the Preschool Student Books, to the Treasure Time Finale. Blow two short blasts on the bamboo whistle, and have children assemble in their Clue Crews. Ask children to hold hands before they leave the room.

Treasure Time Finale
(up to 20 minutes)

Lead children to the room you're using for Treasure Time Finale. The Treasure Time Finale Leader will greet you and show you where to sit.

Preschoolers and older kids will sing songs and then watch someone show love to the Treasure Time Finale Leader...in a surprising way!

When the Treasure Time Finale Leader dismisses everyone, have children remain seated with their Clue Crew Leaders in the Treasure Time Finale area until their parents or caregivers arrive to pick them up. This is a good time for Clue Crew Leaders to collect name badges and put them in the crew treasure bags.

Remind children to take their projects with them when they leave. Be sure to thank parents and caregivers for bringing their children to Treasure Hunt Bible Adventure.

BIBLE POINT

✸ The Bible shows us the way to pray.

BIBLE BASIS

John 17:1–18:11. Jesus prays for his disciples and all believers, and then he is arrested.

We can only imagine the power and peace Jesus drew from his times in prayer. How he must have relished those all-too-brief moments—talking with the Father, pouring out his heart, praying for those he loved, and praising God. Perhaps that's why Jesus so often prayed privately, slipping away from the crowds to spend a few intimate hours with the heavenly Father. But this time was different. After the Passover meal, Jesus prayed, allowing his disciples to hear the burdens of his heart. And although the pain and suffering of the Cross were only hours away, Jesus prayed for his disciples and those they would lead. With his eyes turned toward heaven, Jesus spoke words of love and concern, words of finality and unity. In an intimate moment with the Father, Jesus spoke of those he loved and cared for…including you and me.

Although prayer is a key element in a child's relationship with God, praying can be difficult for children to understand or practice. Since they can't see God, children may feel confused about talking with God or disconnected when they try. That's why the kids at your VBS will appreciate today's activities. They'll learn that God really *does* hear our prayers, that we can use simple words when we pray, and that Jesus loved us so much that he prayed for us. Children will experience meaningful and creative prayers to help them discover the joy of spending time with God.

TREASURE LAND SCHEDULE

LOCATION	ACTIVITY	MINUTES	WHAT CHILDREN WILL DO	CLASSROOM SUPPLIES	PRESCHOOL STUDENT BOOK SUPPLIES
	Treasure Hunt Sing & Play	up to 20	Sing Treasure Hunt Bible Adventure songs with older children.	Name badges, "Bible Point" posters	
Preschool Bible Treasure Land	Report for Adventure!	up to 10	Meet their classmates and get into their Clue Crews.	Name badges	
Preschool Bible Treasure Land	Bible Story Search Party	up to 15	Hunt for the treasure of Jesus' prayers.	Bible, two wrapped boxes, mirror, one copy of "Friends" (p. 72), tempera paint, paintbrushes, butcher paper, baby wipes	
Preschool Bible Treasure Land	Rain Forest Exploration Stations	up to 25	**Option 1: Message Relay**—Pass messages to each other to remember that when we pray, we're sending a message to God.		
			Option 2: Prayer Gloves—Make gloves to remind them of important things to pray about.	Plastic gloves, Treasure Hunt sticker sheets, scissors	
			Option 3: Bible Bookmarks—Create special bookmarks to give to their Bible partners.	Operation Kid-to-Kid Magnetic Bookmarks, markers	
			Option 4: Jesus Prays—Glue fabric scraps to Jesus' robe.	Fabric scraps, glue, scissors	Treasure Land Activity Page: Day 3
	Chadder's Treasure Hunt Theater	up to 15	Hear how Chadder Chipmunk learns the importance of prayer and place the bookmarks and stickers in their partners' Bible books.	Operation Kid-to-Kid Magnetic Bookmarks made earlier, Treasure Hunt sticker sheets, ink pads	Spanish Gospels of John, Preschool Student Book (p. 6)
Preschool Bible Treasure Land	Treasure Treats	up to 15	Eat Prayer Treasure Mix and talk about prayer and prayer requests.	Snacks provided by the Treasure Treats Leader	
	Jungle Gym Playtime Activities	up to 25	**Option 1: Prayer Limbo**—Play a game and learn a chant to remember how special they are to Jesus.	Decorative vines (optional) and a broomstick	
			Option 2: Tube Pass and Praise—Pray for friends in this inner tube game.	Inner tube	
			Option 3: Covered With Prayer—Take special rides to remember the importance of prayer.	Three inner tubes	
			Option 4: Free Play—Enjoy free play outdoors or in the classroom.	Playground equipment, classroom toys, garden hose, funnels, duct tape	
Preschool Bible Treasure Land	Sing-Along Surprise	up to 15	Sing Bible action songs.	Treasure box, mirror, Prayer Gloves, cassette player, *Preschool Bible Treasure Land* audiocassette: "Let Us Pray," "I've Found Me a Treasure," "He's Got the Whole World"	
	Treasure Time Finale	up to 20	Sing songs and watch a skit about prayer.		

Preschool Bible Treasure Land Prep

Before children arrive:

● Choose the Rain Forest Exploration Stations that you'll use, and collect the supplies you'll need.

● Choose which Jungle Gym Playtime Activities options you'll use, and collect the supplies you'll need.

● Choose which Sing-Along Surprise songs you'll use, and cue the *Preschool Bible Treasure Land* audiocassette to the first song you've chosen.

● Consult with the Treasure Treats Leader to find out what time the Treasure Treats Service Crew will deliver your snacks.

● Check with the Treasure Hunt Bible Adventure Director to find out which Jungle Gym Gem will be set up and when preschoolers can use it.

● Photocopy "Friends" from page 72, and tape the picture inside one wrapped box. Place the mirror inside the other wrapped box, and hide both boxes in an area preschoolers can search for them.

Treasure Hunt Sing & Play

(up to 20 minutes)

Before children arrive, arrange with the Treasure Hunt Sing & Play Leader to reserve seats up front for your preschoolers.

Greet children as they arrive. Clue Crew Leaders can give children their name badges and then sit with children and involve them in this sing-along time. Preschoolers will enjoy hearing the music and doing the motions right along with the big kids!

After the Treasure Hunt Sing & Play Leader dismisses your group, have children hold hands in their Clue Crews. Travel together to your Preschool Bible Treasure Land room.

Report for Adventure!

(up to 10 minutes)

After you arrive in your room, make sure each child is wearing his or her name badge.

You can expect new children to visit your Treasure Hunt Bible Adventure each day, so be prepared with extra name badges. Assign new children to Clue Crews.

Blow your bamboo whistle once. Say: **Welcome to Treasure Hunt Bible Adventure! Remember my bamboo whistle? When I blow the bamboo whistle once, it means I want you to look at me.**

Blow the bamboo whistle twice. Ask:

● **Who remembers what two short whistle blasts mean?**

Let children respond. If most of the children were in Treasure Hunt Bible Adventure yesterday, they'll probably remember and may even assemble in their Clue Crews without further instructions.

A CLUE FOR YOU!

If you're using the "rain forest hush" as an attention-getting signal, be sure to practice that too!

Say: **When I blow the bamboo whistle two short times, I want you to quickly gather with your Clue Crew. Let's practice that.** Help children practice finding their crews as you blow the bamboo whistle two short times. Help new children find their assigned crews. If you've hung "Bible Point" posters, lead children to the wall so they can see the posters.

Ask:

● **What did we learn yesterday about what Jesus did for his friends?** (Jesus loved them; Jesus washed their feet; Jesus showed love.)

● **What loving things did you have a chance to do for someone else since yesterday?** (I helped my mom unpack the groceries; I washed dishes; I cleaned my room.)

Say: **Yesterday we heard how Jesus washed his friends' feet. We learned that ✸ the Bible shows us the way to love. Today we're learning that ✸ the Bible shows us the way to pray.** (Eureka!) **Remember to shout "Eureka!" whenever you hear me say, "The Bible shows us the way to pray." "Eureka" means "I found something special!"**

Open your Bible to John 17:1—18:11, and show the passage to children. Say: **Our Bible story is about a very special prayer Jesus prayed. We're going on a treasure hunt to find out what Jesus prayed for. When you're on a treasure hunt, you can find hidden treasures almost anywhere! Sometimes you have to look up.** Look up and encourage children to look up as well. **Sometimes you have to look down.** Look down and have children follow your lead. **Sometimes you have to push aside some plants or look under rocks.** Model these actions. **Sometimes you have to look all around.** Rotate your head in circles.

In this treasure hunt, there are just a couple of rules. First of all, you must stay with your Clue Crew. Second, when you find a treasure, you have to bring it to me so that we can open it together. Ask:

● **Who do you have to stay with?**

● **What do you have to do when you find a treasure?**

Say: **Turn to someone in your Clue Crew and tell the person one place you think a treasure might be hidden.**

Wait a few seconds, and then blow the bamboo whistle once to regain children's attention. Say: ✸ **The Bible shows us the way to pray.** (Eureka!) **Your Clue Crew Leaders will be searching for treasure right along with you today. Stick closely beside them so they don't get distracted!**

Bible Story Search Party

(up to 15 minutes)

Before class, hide the boxes that will help you tell the Bible story, and set out the paint, brushes, butcher paper, and baby wipes in the Bible Story Search Party room.

✸ **BIBLE POINT**
✸ **BIBLE POINT**

Using "Bible Point" posters is not only a super way to decorate your room, but a wonderful means of helping children remember past Bible stories. Preschoolers will be extra delighted to see these bright, colorful posters since they're similar to the artwork in their Preschool Student Books!

- - - - - - -

✸ **BIBLE POINT**

Lead children in the direction of the box that contains the mirror. (It's important that children find the mirror first.) Be sure to use all the search motions you practiced—looking up, down, through bushes, and all around. When a child finds the first treasure box, blow your bamboo whistle to gather children. Let the child who brought you the box open it, and let each child look into the mirror. Ask:

● **Who do you see?** (Me; myself)

● **Why do you think I'm showing you a mirror when we're talking about what Jesus prayed for?** Answers may vary.

Say: **The Bible tells us that in this special prayer time, the first thing Jesus prayed for was himself!** Ask:

● **Have you ever prayed for yourself? What about?** (I prayed that God would make me better; I prayed that God would keep me safe at preschool.)

● **How does it feel to pray for yourself?** (Good; I'm glad that I can.)

Say: **Jesus prayed for himself because what was going to happen to him was very hard. He prayed, "Father, help me." We're going to pray that simple prayer together, just as Jesus did.**

Have all children close their eyes and pray the words, "Father, help me," along with you. Say: **The first thing Jesus prayed for was himself. Let's see if we can find the next treasure to help us discover what else Jesus prayed about.**

Lead children toward the second treasure box. When a child has found it and brought it to you, allow him or her to open it and show the rest of the children the picture of the friends. Ask:

● **What does this picture remind you of?** (My friends; my neighbors.)

● **Tell your crew leader who your best friends are.** Answers will vary.

Allow children to share for a minute, and then blow the bamboo whistle to regain their attention. Say: **Jesus prayed for his friends. They were the people he lived with and loved, and he knew they would need God's help, too. We're going to our Bible Story Search Party room to discover the last thing Jesus prayed about in this special prayer time.**

Lead children inside and have them sit down. Say: **Long ago, way before you were born, Jesus knew about you. He loved you on the day he prayed that special prayer. He prayed for all the men and women and boys and girls who would come to love him today. Look at the front of your hand. See the little tiny lines on each of your fingers? They're different than anyone else's lines. Hold a friend's hand and see how different your friend's fingerprints are from yours.** Allow a few moments for children to compare hands.

Continue: **To help us remember that Jesus prayed for each one of us that day, we're going to make a hand-print mural with the help of our Clue Crew Leaders.**

Have Clue Crew Leaders gently paint the palm of each child's hand; then help children lay their palms on the butcher paper. Instruct crew leaders to

⊗ BIBLE POINT

immediately wipe children's hands with baby wipes. As children are creating the mural, remind them that ⊗ the Bible shows us the way to pray, just as Jesus prayed. Explain that we can pray for ourselves and our friends and always thank Jesus for the love he showed us by praying for us before we were even born. As children finish putting their hand prints on the mural, begin singing "Jesus Loves Me" with them.

When all the children have finished, pray this prayer with them, having children echo each line:

I'll remember to pray for me.
I need your help, I clearly see.
I'll pray for my friends as you showed us to do,
And I'll never forget to say "I love you!"
I love you, Jesus.
Amen.

Put the hand-print mural on the wall where children can reach to touch it during tomorrow's Bible Story Search Party.

RAIN FOREST EXPLORATION STATIONS

(up to 25 minutes)

▼▼ Option 1: MESSAGE RELAY ▼▼▼▼▼▼▼▼▼▼▼▼

1. Have children form a line single-file and then sit down.

2. Whisper a message such as "I like you," "I love to pray," or "I'm glad you're my friend" to the first child in line. Have that child whisper the message to the next child, and continue passing the message down the line.

3. When the message reaches the last child, have him or her say the message out loud. (Children will be interested that sometimes the message isn't right!) Then let that child move to the front of the line and begin a new message.

4. Say: ✿ **The Bible shows us the way to pray. When we pray, it's like passing a message to God. But talking to God is easy—our message always gets through!**

▼▼ Option 2: PRAYER GLOVES ▼▼▼▼▼▼▼▼▼▼▼▼

1. Give each child a plastic glove. Help each child put his or her nondominant hand in the glove. (The fingers will be long, so be sure each finger is pushed all the way into the glove.)

2. Help children remove the "Finger Puppets" stickers from the "Day 3" section of the sticker sheet.

3. Have children spread their fingers wide. Place one sticker on each finger of the glove, loosely wrapping the sticker around.

4. When all the stickers are in place, cut the excess plastic off the fingers of the glove.

5. Help children use their gloves to review the things they can remember to pray for. Point out that ✿ the Bible shows us the way to pray and we can talk to God about anything in the whole world.

▼▼ Option 3: BIBLE BOOKMARKS ▼▼▼▼▼▼▼▼▼▼▼

1. Set out the Operation Kid-to-Kid Magnetic Bookmarks, and explain that children will make this to go into their Spanish Bible books. They'll make a special present for someone they don't even know!

2. Encourage children each to draw themselves on one side of the bookmark and to draw the child who will receive the bookmark on the other side. This is a good opportunity for children to use their imagination!

3. Let children experiment with the magnets to see how they stick together.

4. Say: ✨ **The Bible shows us the way to pray. We can pray for this unknown child, just as Jesus prayed for us. Our prayers draw us together just as the magnets hold the two pictures together.**

If you have enough supplies, you may allow children to make two bookmarks, one to give away and one to keep.

▼▼ Option 4: JESUS PRAYS ▼▼▼▼▼▼▼▼▼▼▼▼▼

1. Give each child the "Treasure Land Activity Page: Day 3" from his or her Preschool Student Book.

2. Set out the fabric scraps, glue, and scissors.

3. Let children glue the fabric scraps to Jesus' robe. Discuss how ✨ the Bible shows us the way to pray by sharing Jesus' prayer with us.

After about twenty-five minutes, blow your bamboo whistle once and announce that it's time for children to clean up their Rain Forest Exploration Stations and get ready to do some more fun things.

When cleanup is complete, blow two short blasts on the bamboo whistle. Wait for children to gather with their Clue Crews and then say: **Now we get to see a video. Remember our friend Chadder Chipmunk? Yesterday Chadder went on a wild ride through a cave! Let's see what kind of adventure is in store for Chadder today on his Treasure Hunt Bible Adventure! Take hold of your friends' hands. We'll travel together to Chadder's Treasure Hunt Theater.**

Chadder's Treasure Hunt Theater

(up to 15 minutes)

Lead children to Chadder's Treasure Hunt Theater. The Chadder's Treasure Hunt Theater Leader will greet you there and show children today's portion of *Chadder's Treasure Hunt Adventure* video.

Say: **Boy, Chadder's in trouble *again!* Tomorrow we'll find out how he gets out of this problem! Whenever we have a problem, we can pray.** ✸ **The Bible shows us the way to pray.** Hold up a Preschool Student Book so children can see the picture on pages 6-7. **Today we learned that Jesus prayed for us before he even knew us. Remember how we looked at the lines on our hands? Whenever you see your hand print or fingerprint, you can remember that Jesus knows everything about you—and he wants to hear your prayers!**

✸ **BIBLE POINT**

To help us remember Jesus' prayers for us, your Clue Crew Leaders will help you stamp your pinkie print onto a sticker. Then you'll put that sticker on this page of your special Bible book.

Distribute ink pads, and have crew leaders help each child make a "pinkie print" on the plain sticker from the "Day 3" section of the sticker sheet. Children may use baby wipes to clean their pinkies and then place the stickers on page 6 of their Student Books.

When everyone has finished, say: **You made some really neat bookmarks to share God's love.** Hold up an Operation Kid-to-Kid Magnetic Bookmark.

Continue: **You've already prayed for your Bible partner while you were making these bookmarks. Now your Clue Crew Leaders will help you place them on a special page of the Spanish Bible book. We'll put the bookmarks near a verse that says God loved us so much that he sent his Son, Jesus. Because God sent Jesus, we can live with God forever in heaven.**

Have Clue Crew Leaders help children find Juan 3:16 in their Spanish Bible books. Let children place the Operation Kid-to-Kid Magnetic Bookmarks on the page. Then have the Clue Crew Leaders collect the Preschool Student Books.

Say: **Let's get into our Clue Crews and hold hands as we travel for our Treasure Treats time.**

Treasure Treats
(up to 15 minutes)

> # Prayer Trail Mix
>
> **Pretzels** look like folded hands, and they remind us to pray.
>
> **Cheerios** cereal is little circles that have no beginning and no end. It reminds us of God's never-ending love.
>
> **Life** cereal reminds us to be thankful for God's gift of life.
>
> **M&M's** candies are sweet and good. They stand for God's sweet, good blessings—the wonderful gifts God gives us.
>
> **Goldfish** crackers remind us that God provides the things we need, such as food.
>
> **Gummy bears** look a little bit like the stained-glass windows that some churches have. They remind us to thank God for churches, where we go to learn about him.

Field Test Findings

During the field test, we noticed that children were so busy that their Clue Crew Leaders hardly had time to get to know each child. By asking getting-to-know-you questions during snack time, the leaders were able to make long-term connections with each little person! What a blessing!

Return to your room, and have children sit down at tables or in another eating area. Use the key above to explain the significance of each part of the snack. Have children pick up a piece of the trail mix as you describe it. Ask volunteers to say a short prayer for each item represented in the trail mix. You'll be surprised how adept these little ones can be at expressing their thoughts to God!

As children enjoy the snack, have Clue Crew Leaders talk with their children about their prayer experiences and requests.

When children finish their snacks, have them throw away their napkins and cups. Then blow two short blasts on the bamboo whistle, and have children assemble in their Clue Crews.

Jungle Gym Playtime Activities
(up to 25 minutes)

If you choose to go outdoors for playtime, you may want to intersperse unstructured play with some or all of the following activities. If you remain indoors, let children revisit their favorite Rain Forest Exploration Stations or let them engage in unstructured play. (Some of the following activities may also be appropriate for your indoor area. Use your discretion when choosing safe activities for indoor Jungle Gym Playtime Activities.)

Option 1: Prayer Limbo
Create a limbo stick by wrapping a broomstick with decorative vines. Have two leaders hold on to the limbo stick. Start it out at the leaders' shoulder height, and have the crews pass under it as you all learn this chant in classic limbo rhythm.

Jesus prayed for you—YOU.

Jesus prayed for me—TOO!
The Bible shows us how—HOW
To pray about things now—NOW!

Vary the tempo and the volume of the chant, and try to get children to move accordingly. Keep lowering the pole until children are crawling under. No one gets out in this game! Everyone's a winner!

Option 2: Tube Pass and Praise

Have children stand in a circle. Demonstrate how to roll the inner tube on its edge. Roll the tube to a child across the circle as you say, "Thank you, God, for my friend [name]!" When that child catches the tube, he or she can roll it to another friend until everyone has had a turn. Say: ✸ **The Bible shows us the way to pray.** (Eureka!). **It's good to pray for our friends.**

✸ **BIBLE POINT**

Option 3: Covered With Prayer

Have three inner tubes ready to place over a child's head as you sing this song to the tune of "Bingo":

Step inside this special ride
To help you to remember:
Jesus prayed for you. (Place the first tube.)
Others are praying, too. (Place the second tube.)
As the Bible shows us to,
We pray for one another. (Place the third tube.)

Carefully tip the child over inside the tubes, and roll the child several feet forward! Before the child gets out of the tubes, say: ✸ **The Bible shows us the way to pray.** (Eureka!)

✸ **BIBLE POINT**

Field Test Findings

We probably had as much fun watching this activity as children had doing it! The children loved tipping over and bouncing in the inner tubes!

Option 4: Free Play

Before playtime, use duct tape to secure a funnel on each end of a garden hose. Have two children stand where they can't see each other and take turns talking and listening through the funnels. Point out that even though we can't see God he hears us clearly just as we can hear the people talking on the tube phone.

If you're outdoors, let children play with outdoor toys such as balls or soap bubbles or use chalk on the sidewalk. Children would also enjoy outdoor playground equipment if it's available. If you're indoors, let children play with classroom toys such as blocks, stuffed animals, or modeling dough. As children play, look for opportunities to review today's Bible Point and Bible story.

After about twenty minutes, blow the bamboo whistle once to let children know it's time to finish their activities and clean up. If you're outside, blow the bamboo whistle twice after cleanup is complete to signal your return to the classroom. Then gather in the story area for singing.

Sing-Along Surprise

(up to 15 minutes)

The special treasure today is a mirror. Ask: **Are you ready for the special treasure riddle for today?**

Say:

Is it you, or is it me?

Take a look! Let's see!

First it's you; now it's me!

Tell me now, how could this be?

Let children try to guess. If they need clues, remind them about the Bible story item that allowed each person to see himself or herself.

✸ BIBLE POINT

Say: ✸ **The Bible shows us the way to pray.** (Eureka!) **Let's look at our prayer gloves and see if we can find some special things to pray about.** Let children tell you about the stickers on their gloves. Ask:

● **Are there things that are not on your prayer glove that you might want to pray about? What are those things?** (My dog; my church, my teacher.)

● **Why do you think prayer is like a treasure?** (It's valuable; it's special.)

Say: **Let's sing some songs to help us think about all the great things the Bible shows us the way to do!** Lead children in singing one or more of the following songs.

Let Us Pray

Let us pray, let us pray *(bring praying hands together overhead and then bring them down in front)*

Everywhere and every way *(move praying hands to left shoulder and then to right shoulder),*

Every moment of the day. *(Point to imaginary watch on wrist.)*

It is the right time. *(Make the "OK" sign.)*

For the Father above *(hold arms overhead, palms up, and look up),*

He is listening with love (*hold hands behind ears on "listening" and then cross arms over chest*);

And he wants to answer us (*extend arms in front and then to sides*),

So let us pray. (*Hold prayer hands in front.*)

Yeah, yeah, yeah. (*Hold prayer hands and turn a complete circle.*)

Let us pray, let us pray (*bring praying hands together overhead and then bring them down in front*)

Everywhere and every way (*move praying hands to left shoulder and then to right shoulder*),

Every moment of the day. (*Point to imaginary watch on wrist.*)

It is the right time. (*Make the "OK" sign.*)

For the Father above (*hold arms overhead, palms up, and look up*),

He is listening with love (*hold hands behind ears on "listening" and then cross arms over chest*);

And he wants to answer us (*extend arms in front and then to sides*),

So let us pray. (*Hold prayer hands in front.*)

Yeah, yeah, yeah. (*Hold prayer hands and turn a complete circle.*)

Let us pray, let us pray (*bring praying hands together overhead and then bring them down in front*)

Everywhere and every way (*move praying hands to left shoulder and then to right shoulder*),

Every moment of the day. (*Point to imaginary watch on wrist.*)

It is the right time. (*Make the "OK" sign.*)

For the Father above (*hold arms overhead, palms up, and look up*),

He is listening with love (*hold hands behind ears on "listening" and then cross arms over chest*);

And he wants to answer us (*extend arms in front and then to sides*),

So let us pray. (*Hold prayer hands in front.*)

Yeah, yeah, yeah, yeah. (*Hold prayer hands and turn a complete circle.*)

I've Found Me a Treasure (Day 3)

Chorus:

I've found me a treasure (*put hands next to mouth as if shouting and bounce from right to left with the beat*);

I've found a friend. (*Keep hands next to mouth and bounce from left to right.*)

I found Jesus (*sign "Jesus"*),

And his love will never end. (*Cross arms over chest on "love," extend right arm to side on "never," and extend left arm to side on "end."*)

I've found me a treasure (*put hands next to mouth as if shouting and bounce from*

right to left with the beat);
I've found a friend. (Keep hands next to mouth and bounce from left to right.)
I found Jesus (sign "Jesus"),
And his love will never end. (Cross arms over chest on "love," extend right arm to side on "never," and extend left arm to side on "end.")

Day 3:
Jesus, speaking in a garden (put hands next to mouth),
Showed us how to pray. (Make prayer hands.)
Bow your head, get on your knees (put hands on top of head, and then pat knees)—
Just ask it in his name. (Raise arms overhead.)

(Repeat chorus)

He's Got the Whole World in His Hands

He's got the whole world (sweep arms up and around in a big circle)
In his hands. (Hold out one hand, palm up, and then cup the other hand in the first.)
He's got the whole world (sweep arms up and around in a big circle)
In his hands. (Hold out one hand, palm up, and then cup the other hand in the first.)
He's got the whole world (sweep arms up and around in a big circle)
In his hands. (Hold out one hand, palm up, and then cup the other hand in the first.)
He's got the whole world (sweep arms up and around in a big circle)
In his hands. (Hold out one hand, palm up, and then cup the other hand in the first.)

He's got the wind and the rain (sweep hands from side to side for "wind," and then wiggle fingers down for "rain.")
In his hands. (Hold out one hand, palm up, and then cup the other hand in the first.)
He's got the wind and the rain (sweep hands from side to side for "wind," and then wiggle fingers down for "rain.")
In his hands. (Hold out one hand, palm up, and then cup the other hand in the first.)
He's got the wind and the rain (sweep hands from side to side for "wind," and then wiggle fingers down for "rain.")
In his hands. (Hold out one hand, palm up, and then cup the other hand in the first.)
He's got the whole world (sweep arms up and around in a big circle)
In his hands. (Hold out one hand, palm up, and then cup the other hand in the first.)

He's got everybody here (point to others)
In his hands. (Hold out one hand, palm up, and then cup the other hand in the first.)
He's got everybody here (point to others)

In his hands. *(Hold out one hand, palm up, and then cup the other hand in the first.)*
He's got everybody here *(point to others)*
In his hands. *(Hold out one hand, palm up, and then cup the other hand in the first.)*
He's got the whole world *(sweep arms up and around in a big circle)*
In his hands. *(Hold out one hand, palm up, and then cup the other hand in the first.)*

Have children stand up in a circle to do this song together.

Prayer Pokey

(Sing to the tune of "Hokey Pokey.")

You put your right foot in; you take your right foot out.
You put your right foot in, and you shake it all about.
You want to be like Jesus, so you sit yourself right down. *(Drop down to your knees.)*
Prayer is what it's all about. *(Place your palms together; then raise your arms up high.)*
Whoo!

Have children get up and repeat the song with left foot, right hand, left hand, and whole self.

After the last song, have Clue Crew Leaders collect any Rain Forest Exploration Station projects they don't have in their treasure bags. Then blow two short blasts on the bamboo whistle, and have children assemble in their Clue Crews. Have everyone hold hands before they leave your room.

Treasure Time Finale
(up to 20 minutes)

Lead children to the room you are using for Treasure Time Finale. The Treasure Time Finale Leader will greet you and show you where to sit.

Preschoolers and older kids will sing songs and then watch a fun skit about what it really means to pray.

When the Treasure Time Finale Leader dismisses everyone, have children remain seated with their Clue Crew Leaders in the Treasure Time Finale area until their parents or caregivers arrive to pick them up. This is a good time to have Clue Crew Leaders collect name badges and place them in their crew treasure bags.

Remind children to take their projects with them when they leave. Be sure to thank parents and caregivers for bringing their children to Treasure Hunt Bible Adventure.

FRIENDS

DAY 4

BIBLE POINT

The Bible shows us the way to Jesus.

BIBLE BASIS

John 19:1–20:18. Jesus is crucified, rises again, and appears to Mary Magdalene.

Jesus' crucifixion was both a devastating and defining event for his followers. Although Peter, a close friend and disciple, denied knowing Jesus, Joseph of Arimathea and Nicodemus, who had been secret followers, came forward in their faith to bury Jesus. Even Mary Magdalene thought she'd lost her greatest treasure. Seeing the empty tomb, Mary probably assumed someone had stolen Jesus' body. Through her tears, she told the angels, "They have taken my Lord away, and I don't know where they have put him." Jesus, her treasure, was gone, and more than anything Mary wanted to find him. Mary didn't need to search for long. Jesus lovingly called her name, revealing himself and the miracle of his resurrection.

The greatest treasure children can find is Jesus. For in knowing Jesus, children will experience forgiveness, love, and eternal life. However, like Mary, the kids at your VBS may have trouble "seeing" Jesus. Mixed messages from the media, school, and non-Christian friends may confuse kids or mislead them. But just as Jesus called Mary by name, Jesus calls each of us by name, too. He knows the hearts and minds of the children at your VBS. Today's activities will help children discover that Jesus is the greatest treasure of all, and that he's right there, waiting for them with open arms.

TREASURE LAND SCHEDULE

LOCATION	ACTIVITY	MINUTES	WHAT CHILDREN WILL DO	CLASSROOM SUPPLIES	PRESCHOOL STUDENT BOOK SUPPLIES
Preschool Bible Treasure Land	Treasure Hunt Sing & Play	up to 20	Sing Treasure Hunt Bible Adventure songs with older children.	Name badges	
Preschool Bible Treasure Land	Report for Adventure!	up to 10	Meet their classmates and get into their Clue Crews.	Name badges, "Bible Point" posters	
Preschool Bible Treasure Land	Bible Story Search Party	up to 15	Hear how Mary Magdalene recognized Jesus when he called her name.	Bible, two bedsheets or Bible-time costumes, hand-print mural from Day 3, flashlight, an assistant to play the part of Jesus or Mary	
Preschool Bible Treasure Land	Rain Forest Exploration Stations	up to 25	**Option 1: Out-of-the-Tomb Puppets**—Make pop-up puppets to reinforce the fact that Jesus came out of the tomb alive!	Foam cups, tissues, craft sticks, newsprint, Treasure Hunt sticker sheets	Treasure Land Activity Page: Day 4
			Option 2: Name Treasures—Decorate treasure necklaces with their names.	Index cards, permanent marker, glue-on gems, Treasure Hunt sticker sheets, craft glue, hole punch, yarn, scissors	
			Option 3: Treasure Pouches—Make their own permanent pouches to hold their treasures.	Good News Treasure Pouches, Mini Jungle Vine, Hershey's Kisses candies	
			Option 4: Mary Finds Jesus—Create a picture that shows how Mary went from sad to happy when she saw Jesus.	Scissors, crayons, Treasure Hunt sticker sheets	
	Chadder's Treasure Hunt Theater	up to 15	See how Chadder Chipmunk discovers a valuable treasure; then mark their Bible books so they'll know where to find the greatest treasure of all.	Supplies provided by Chadder's Treasure Hunt Theater Leader, Treasure Hunt sticker sheets	Preschool Student Books (pp. 8-9), Spanish Gospels of John
Preschool Bible Treasure Land	Treasure Treats	up to 15	Eat Empty Tombs and talk about people who have helped them learn about Jesus.	Snacks provided by the Treasure Treats Leader	
	Jungle Gym Playtime Activities	up to 25	**Option 1: Tomb Tunnel**—Play angels and hide in a tunnel until called out.	Garbage can tunnel, flashlight, inner tube	
			Option 2: Name Rover—Play a Red Rover-style game and listen for their names.		
			Option 3: Jungle Obstacle Course—Follow arrows through the course and learn how the Bible shows us the way to Jesus.	Garbage can tunnel, inner tubes, broomstick, masking tape, Bibles, index cards, marker	
			Option 4: Free Play—Enjoy free play outdoors or in the classroom.	Playground equipment, classroom toys, masking tape	
Preschool Bible Treasure Land	Sing-Along Surprise	up to 15	Sing Bible action songs.	Treasure box, cassette player, Preschool Bible Treasure Land audiocassette: "He's Alive," "I've Found Me a Treasure," "Good News"	
	Treasure Time Finale	up to 20	Sing songs and watch as "Jesus" makes their "sins" disappear.		

Preschool Bible Treasure Land Prep

Before children arrive:

● Choose which Rain Forest Exploration Stations you'll use, and collect the supplies you'll need.

● Choose which Jungle Gym Playtime Activities options you'll use, and collect the supplies you'll need.

● Choose which Sing-Along Surprise songs you'll use.

● Consult with the Treasure Treats Leader to find out what time the Treasure Treats Service Crew will deliver your snacks.

● Prepare a sample Treasure Pouch according to the directions on page 79.

Treasure Hunt Sing & Play

(up to 20 minutes)

Before children arrive, arrange with the Treasure Hunt Sing & Play Leader to reserve seats up front for your preschoolers.

Greet children as they arrive. Clue Crew Leaders can give children their name badges and then sit with children and involve them in this sing-along time. Preschoolers will enjoy hearing the music and doing the motions right along with the big kids!

After the Treasure Hunt Sing & Play Leader dismisses your group, have children hold hands in their Clue Crews. Travel together to your Preschool Bible Treasure Land room.

Report for Adventure!

(up to 10 minutes)

After you arrive in your room, make sure each child is wearing his or her name badge.

You can expect new children to visit your Treasure Hunt Bible Adventure each day, so be prepared with extra name badges. Assign new children to Clue Crews.

Blow your bamboo whistle once. Say: **Welcome to Treasure Hunt Bible Adventure! Remember my bamboo whistle? When I blow the bamboo whistle once, it means I want you to look at me.**

Blow the bamboo whistle twice. Ask:

● **Who remembers what two short bamboo whistle blasts mean?**

Let children respond. If most of the children were in Treasure Hunt Bible Adventure yesterday, they'll probably remember and may even assemble in their Clue Crews without further instructions.

Say: **When I blow the bamboo whistle two short times, I want you to quickly gather with your Clue Crew. Let's practice that.** Help children practice finding their crews as you blow the bamboo whistle two short times. Help new children find their assigned crews. Point to the "Bible

A CLUE FOR YOU!

While preschoolers may not understand all the implications of Jesus' death and resurrection, they *can* understand the fact that Jesus loves them enough to give his life for them. It's never too early to teach the basic gospel message of God's love!

A CLUE FOR YOU!

If you choose to make the Treasure Names, cut several sixteen- to twenty-inch lengths of yarn ahead of time. You may want to write "is a treasure to Jesus" along the bottom of each index card, as well. This simple prep will make this center go more smoothly.

A CLUE FOR YOU!

For the Name Treasures activity, children can also use extra gem stickers from the "Surprise Treasure Chest" section of their sticker sheets.

Point" posters, and say: **Yesterday we heard how Jesus prayed for him-self, his friends, and *you!* ✸ The Bible shows us the way to pray. Today we're learning that ✸ The Bible shows us the way to Jesus.** (Eureka!) **Our Bible story is about Jesus' friend named Mary.**

It's important for us to know that before our story begins, Jesus died on the cross. They took his body from the cross and placed it in a cave or a tomb to be his grave. They rolled a huge stone in front of the door of the tomb. All of Jesus' friends were very sad. Ask:

● **How would you feel if you thought you would never see your best friend again?** (Very sad; I'd cry.)

● **What are some things people do when someone they love dies?** (Cry; have a funeral; give flowers.)

Say: **Jesus' friends may have felt that way and done some of those things, too. Another thing they did was go to his tomb to take care of his body. Let's take a trip to remember his tomb and to find out what happened there.**

Bible Story Search Party

(up to 15 minutes)

Have the Clue Crew Leaders lead children on a trip while you dress as your Bible character. Have your assistant get into costume, as well. Be sure to set up the flashlight so that it will illuminate the face of "Jesus" when it's turned on. Make sure "Jesus" knows children's names, or provide a list so that everyone's name can be called. When children arrive at the designated story area, "Mary" should enter the room in character.

Say: **Jesus knows each one of your names, and he loves you very much. Remember he was thinking about you before you were even born. He prayed for you, and he died because he loved you.** Begin to sing: **Yes, Jesus loves me. Yes, Jesus loves me. Yes, Jesus loves me. The Bible tells me so.** Sing slowly, reflectively, and reverently to lead children in a moment of worship and adoration. Then sing the chorus to "Oh, How I Love Jesus," continuing the mood of worship. At this point, "Jesus" could hug children before leaving the room.

Help children locate their own hand print on the mural they created yes-terday. Say: **Even though it may be hard for us to remember our very own hand prints from one day to the next, Jesus will always remem-ber us, love us, and call out our names to ask us to follow him. Jesus is a precious treasure to us, and we are a precious treasure to him. And ✸ the Bible shows us the way to Jesus.** (Eureka!)

MARY: *(Weeping)* My name is Mary. Jesus was my best friend. I never knew anyone like him. He knew every bad thing I'd ever done, and he loved me anyway. He loved everyone. He loved people so much that he prayed for children and grown-ups who weren't even born yet, like the children who left their hand prints on that wall over there. *(Point to the hand-print mural.)* I came here to care for his body, but I can't find it. *(Weeping softly)* Do you know where Jesus' body is? We laid him in the tomb over there, but now he's gone! Please tell me if you know who took his body. *(Plead a bit more with the children to tell you where Jesus is, and look where they suggest to look.)*

(Jesus enters room and stands at a distance.)

MARY: *(Seeing Jesus)* Please, sir, if you know where they've taken my Lord's body, please tell me.

JESUS: Mary! *(Turn on the hidden flashlight to light up your face.)*

MARY: *(Dropping to knees in worship)* Master! *(Turning to children)* It's him! It's him. As soon as I heard him say my name, I knew it was him. He isn't dead! He's alive! And he knows my name. He knows your name too! Listen!

(Jesus approaches children. He says the name of each child and reaches out to touch each one's hands. The children may or may not want to reach their hands up to touch him.)

Field Test Findings

All the adults in the room were moved to tears by our children's reaction to Jesus and the worshipful singing that followed. It was truly a blessed experience for all of us.

Field Test Findings

We discovered that the Jesus character was powerful (and maybe a little intimidating) to children! Many were a little hesitant to reach their hands to him. Try to make your Jesus as gentle and "touchable" as possible so every child can have this meaningful experience. (The act of touching and calling each child by name was also a powerful experience for the person portraying Jesus!)

RAIN FOREST EXPLORATION STATIONS

(up to 25 minutes)

▼▼ Option 1: OUT-OF-THE-TOMB PUPPETS ▼▼▼▼

1. Give each child a craft stick, a tissue, and a foam cup.

2. Show children how to lay the tissue out flat over the nondominant hand.

3. Then have each child pick up a craft stick, point it into the tissue-covered palm, and flip his or her hand over to cover the stick with the tissue. Help each child gently push the stick through the tissue until about one-half inch of the stick is showing.

4. Help each child place the "Pop-Up Puppet" sticker from the "Day 4" section over both the stick and part of the tissue to secure them.

5. Help children poke the craft sticks into the bottoms of the foam cups and then place the Jesus puppets all the way down inside the cups so that the sticks poke out the bottom.

6. Have each child crumple newsprint to form a rock to put over the opening of the "tomb."

7. Children can use the craft sticks to push the puppets up, dislodging the rocks and saying, "He is risen!" Talk about how  the Bible shows us the way to Jesus. Then each cup can be turned over, and the craft stick placed in the bottom of the cup to form a base for the living Jesus.

▼▼ Option 2: NAME TREASURES ▼▼▼▼▼▼▼▼▼

1. Set the gems, index cards, and craft glue on the table.

2. Give each child an index card. As you distribute the cards, use a permanent marker to write each child's name on his or her card. Add the words "is a treasure to Jesus" on the bottom of each card, if you haven't already done so.

3. Let children add several gems to their name tags. Then help each child punch a hole in the top center of the card.

4. Cut a piece of yarn long enough to hang the card around the child's neck.

5. Be sure to read aloud each child's name tag. Reinforce that Jesus knows their names and that  the Bible shows us the way to Jesus.

Field Test Findings

We thought it would be great fun to have children trace their names with glitter glue. However, we found that the glitter glue came out too fast for little hands to control!

RAIN FOREST EXPLORATION STATIONS

▼▼ Option 3: TREASURE POUCHES ▼▼▼▼▼▼▼▼▼▼

1. Give each child a flat Good News Treasure Pouch and a two-foot length of Mini Jungle Vine.

2. Have children place the pouch so the plastic side is facing up. Show them how to weave the Mini Jungle Vine in and out of the holes.

3. As children weave the pouches, help them "scrunch" the material at the top, pushing the plastic side down inside the pouch. When children have finished weaving around the pouch, tie the ends of their Mini Jungle Vines together to create necklaces.

4. Give each child several Hershey's Kisses candies to put in his or her pouch.

Ask children what other treasures they might put into their pouches. Reinforce that the best treasure of all can't be stored in a pouch. It's Jesus— and  the Bible shows us the way to Jesus.

▼▼ Option 4: MARY FINDS JESUS ▼▼▼▼▼▼▼▼▼▼

1. Have Clue Crew Leaders tear out the "Treasure Land Activity Page: Day 4" from each child's Preschool Student Book.

2. Cut along the dotted lines at the top and bottom of Mary Magdalene's face. Help children cut off the strip at the bottom of the page. (Children can begin to color the pictures while you do this.)

3. Help children place the stickers from the "Day 4" section of the sticker sheet on the paper strip. Thread the strip through the slits so children can watch Mary's face change from sad to happy.

4. Remind children that the Bible is a special treasure because ✸ the Bible shows us the way to Jesus.

After about twenty-five minutes, blow your bamboo whistle once and announce that it's time for children to clean up their Rain Forest Exploration Stations and get ready to do some more fun things.

When cleanup is complete, blow two short blasts on the bamboo whistle. Wait for children to gather with their Clue Crews, and then say: **Now we get to go see a video. Remember our friend, Chadder the chipmunk? Yesterday he met lots of new friends. Take hold of your friends' hands. We'll travel together to Chadder's Treasure Hunt Theater.**

Chadder's Treasure Hunt Theater

(up to 15 minutes)

Lead children to Chadder's Treasure Hunt Theater. The Chadder's Treasure Hunt Theater Leader will greet you there and show children today's portion of *Chadder's Treasure Hunt Adventure* video.

⊛ BIBLE POINT

Say: **Wow! I wonder what will happen to Chadder! Even though Chadder discovered gold and gems, he also knows that ⊛ the Bible shows us the way to Jesus.** (Eureka!) **And Jesus is the greatest treasure of all! Let's take a minute and put a sticker in our Bible books that will help us find Jesus.**

Hold up a Preschool Student Book so children can see the picture on pages 8-9. Continue: **On many treasure hunts, X marks the spot where you'll find the treasure. If you turn an X on its side, it looks like a cross. A cross shows us how much Jesus loves us—so much that he died on a cross for all the bad things we've done! Let's put an "X" sticker in our Bible books to show us that this story marks the spot where we find Jesus!**

Have Clue Crew Leaders help children place the large "X" stickers on page 8 of their Bible books. When children have finished, say: **We want our Spanish-speaking Bible partners to find the treasure of Jesus, too. Let's put the "X" sticker in their Bibles.** Have Clue Crew Leaders help children place the smaller "X" stickers on the pages of the Spanish Bible books to mark John 3:16. Then say: **To make sure that our Spanish-speaking Bible partners know about the treasure of Jesus, your Clue Crew Leaders will highlight the verse I told you about yesterday. This verse tells us that God sent Jesus to die to take away all the bad things we've done.** Distribute highlighters, and show Clue Crew Leaders where to find John 3:16 in the Spanish Gospels of John.

When each Bible has been marked and returned to the crew treasure bags, say: **Now we have good reminders that X marks the spot where we find Jesus—the greatest treasure ever! Let's hold hands as we travel back to Preschool Bible Treasure Land.**

Treasure Treats

(up to 15 minutes)

Return to your room, and have children sit down at tables or in another eating area. Show children an Empty Tomb snack. Point out that when you roll the

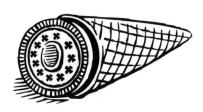

cookie "stone" away from the cone, the "tomb" is empty! Then give each child a napkin, an Empty Tomb, and a cup half-filled with water. Keep a supply of paper towels handy to wipe up any spills.

As children enjoy the snack, have Clue Crew Leaders ask them about people who have helped them learn about Jesus.

When children finish their snacks, have them throw away their napkins and cups. Then blow two short blasts on the bamboo whistle, and have children assemble in their Clue Crews.

Jungle Gym Playtime Activities
(up to 25 minutes)

If you choose to go outdoors for playtime, you may want to intersperse unstructured play with some or all of the following activities. If you remain indoors, let children revisit their favorite Rain Forest Exploration Stations, or let them engage in unstructured play. (Some of the following activities may also be appropriate for your indoor area. Use your discretion when choosing safe activities for indoor Jungle Gym Playtime Activities.)

Option 1: Tomb Tunnel

Set out the garbage can "tunnel" along with a flashlight and an inner tube.

Gather children in a circle around the tunnel, and choose a child to be the Angel. Have this child climb inside the tunnel tomb. He or she can turn on the flashlight inside the tunnel. Cover the opening with the inner tube. Have the rest of the children call, "One, two, three—where could Jesus be?" The child inside the tunnel will pop out and yell back, "He isn't here! He's risen!" As soon as the Angel pops out, the rest of the children can run around the circle as though they're running to tell their friends. When the Clue Crew Leader calls out a name, everyone will freeze, and the child whose name was called will become the new Angel.

Option 2: Name Rover

Have children line up in two parallel lines several feet apart. Have one crew decide who to call from the other crew. Then have them say this chant, inserting the chosen child's name, "Never fear, never fear. Send our friend [name] over here!" Remind children that Jesus calls each one of us to come to him and the Bible shows us the way to Jesus.

⚘ BIBLE POINT

Option 3: Jungle Obstacle Course

Use all your available props to set up an obstacle course. Have children crawl through the tunnel, walk around inner tubes, jump over a broomstick, or crawl between narrowly placed masking tape lines. Use your imagination to create a fun and challenging course. Between each prop, place a Bible that has an arrow drawn on an index card pointing to the next obstacle. Remind children that the Bible can be depended on to give us direction and ⚘ the Bible shows us the way to Jesus.

⚘ BIBLE POINT

Option 4: Free Play

If you're outdoors, let children play with outdoor toys such as balls and soap bubbles or use chalk on the sidewalk. Children would also enjoy outdoor playground equipment if it's available. If you're indoors, let children play with classroom toys such as blocks, stuffed animals, or modeling dough. As children play, look for opportunities to review today's Bible Point and Bible story. In addition to the usual toys, consider laying several masking tape lines on the ground for preschoolers to balance on as though they were vine bridges through the rain forest.

After about twenty minutes, blow the bamboo whistle once to let children know it's time to finish their activities and clean up. If you're outside, blow the bamboo whistle twice after cleanup is complete to signal your return to the classroom. Then gather in the story area for singing.

Sing-Along Surprise
(up to 15 minutes)

Today the treasure box will be empty to remind children of the empty tomb. Say: **What a great day we've had together! Are you ready to find out what the special surprise is today? Would anyone like to guess before I give the clue?**

Here's today's riddle.
I'm not small, and I'm not big.
I'm what you'd find in a hole you dig.

Have children make holes by holding their index fingers and thumbs together. Ask children what's inside the holes their fingers made.

Open the box, and let all the children look inside. Ask:

● **How could nothing be a treasure?**

Say: **The empty box reminds us of the empty tomb! One of God's** biggest treasures for us is that Jesus is alive! We can't find Jesus in a tomb because he's alive! But ✳ the Bible shows us the way to Jesus. (Eureka!) **We find him as we read and hear about him, and as we listen for him to call our names!** Ask:

● **What was your favorite activity today?** (Being an angel; playing the game.)

● **How does that help you to remember Jesus and his love for you?** (Jesus died for me; Jesus knows my name.)

Say: **Let's sing some songs together to remind us that ✳ the Bible shows us the way to Jesus.** (Eureka!)

Lead children in singing one or more of the following songs.

He's Alive

He is alive. *(Lift shoulders, alternating with each beat, while bouncing knees.)* *(Clap with the rhythm.)*
He is alive. *(Lift shoulders, alternating with each beat, while bouncing knees.)* *(Clap with the rhythm.)*
I can see *(hop so right side faces forward, and then "surf")*
Above the clouds *(hop so left side faces forward, and then "surf"),*
And I can hear him *(hop so right side faces forward, and then "surf")*
Call my name out loud. *(Hop so left side faces forward, and then "surf.")* *(Clap with the rhythm.)*

He is alive. *(Lift shoulders, alternating with each beat, while bouncing knees.)* *(Clap with the rhythm.)*
He is alive. *(Lift shoulders, alternating with each beat, while bouncing knees.)* *(Clap with the rhythm.)*
He has come that *(hop so right side faces forward, and then "surf")*
I might have life *(hop so left side faces forward, and then "surf"),*
And more life than *(hop so right side faces forward, and then "surf")*
I have had before. *(Hop so left side faces forward, and then "surf.")* *(Clap with the rhythm.)*

He is alive. *(Lift shoulders, alternating with each beat, while bouncing knees.)* *(Clap with the rhythm.)*
He is alive. *(Lift shoulders, alternating with each beat, while bouncing knees.)* *(Clap with the rhythm.)*
He is alive. *(Lift shoulders, alternating with each beat, while bouncing knees.)* *(Clap with the rhythm.)*

I've Found Me a Treasure (Day 4)

Chorus:

I've found me a treasure *(put hands next to mouth as if shouting and bounce from right to left with the beat);*

I've found a friend. *(Keep hands next to mouth and bounce from left to right.)*

I found Jesus *(sign "Jesus"),*

And his love will never end. *(Cross arms over chest on "love," extend right arm to side on "never," and extend left arm to side on "end.")*

I've found me a treasure *(put hands next to mouth as if shouting and bounce from right to left with the beat);*

I've found a friend. *(Keep hands next to mouth and bounce from left to right.)*

I found Jesus *(sign "Jesus"),*

And his love will never end. *(Cross arms over chest on "love," extend right arm to side on "never," and extend left arm to side on "end.")*

Day 4:

For God, he so loved the world *(raise arms overhead, and then cross arms over chest)*

That he gave his only Son *(sign "Jesus")*

That we may have eternal life. *(Raise arms overhead.)*

We are the chosen ones. *(Keep hands raised and shake "praise" hands with the beat.)*

(Repeat chorus)

Good News

(Snap to the beat.)

Good news! *(Point with right hand, then left.)*

Jesus was born. *(Rock imaginary baby.)*

Good news! *(Point with right hand, then left.)*

He died on the cross. *(Raise arms, and then bring them down to sides.)*

Good news! *(Point with right hand, then left.)*

He rose again. *(Raise arms.)*

Good news! *(Point with right hand, then left.)*

He's coming back soon. *(Motion "come here" with right arm.)*

(Snap to the beat.)

Good news! *(Point with right hand, then left.)*

Jesus was born. *(Rock imaginary baby.)*

Good news! *(Point with right hand, then left.)*

He died on the cross. *(Raise arms, and then bring them down to sides.)*

Good news! *(Point with right hand, then left.)*

He rose again. *(Raise arms.)*
Good news! *(Point with right hand, then left.)*
He's coming back soon. *(Motion "come here" with right arm.)*

(Either march in place or do a box step during the verse.)
God sent Jesus,
His only Son,
To save me from my sin.
He's the only one
Who can change my heart
And make me his own.
He saved me *(jump in place);*
He loves me *(jump in place);*
My heart is his home. *(Hug self and twist.)*

Good news! *(Point with right hand, then left.)*
Jesus was born. *(Rock imaginary baby.)*
Good news! *(Point with right hand, then left.)*
He died on the cross. *(Raise arms, and then bring them down to sides.)*
Good news! *(Point with right hand, then left.)*
He rose again. *(Raise arms.)*
Good news! *(Point with right hand, then left.)*
He's coming back soon. *(Motion "come here" with right arm.)*

(Snap to the beat.)
Good news! *(Point with right hand, then left.)*
Jesus was born. *(Rock imaginary baby.)*
Good news! *(Point with right hand, then left.)*
He died on the cross. *(Raise arms, and then bring them down to sides.)*
Good news! *(Point with right hand, then left.)*
He rose again. *(Raise arms.)*
Good news! *(Point with right hand, then left.)*
He's coming back soon. *(Motion "come here" with right arm.)*

If time allows, you may wish to teach children this finger play to use with their Treasure Pouches. If you didn't make Treasure Pouches, give each child several Hershey's Kisses candies at the end of the finger play.

One greedy little monkey tried to sneak away *(hold up your index finger)*
With a very special treasure he found one fine spring day.
His tiny little brother *(hold up the pinkie of your other hand)*
Longed to share in all the fun,
But he could never catch up with brother number one. *(Have your*
pinkie chase the index finger.)

Along came mother monkey to remind the little pair *(wiggle your two thumbs together)*

That every treasure's better when that treasure's shared. *(Touch pinkie and index finger together while keeping thumbs together.)*

Ask:

● **Who could you share your candy treasure with?** (My big brother; my mom; my neighbor.)

● **Who could you share the treasure of Jesus with?** (Everyone; my dad; my sister; my friends.)

Encourage children to act on their ideas, and repeat the finger play for emphasis.

After the finger play, have Clue Crew Leaders collect their children's projects. Then blow two short blasts on the bamboo whistle, and have children assemble in their Clue Crews. Have everyone hold hands before they leave your room.

Treasure Time Finale

(up to 20 minutes)

Lead children to the room you're using for Treasure Time Finale. The Treasure Time Finale Leader will greet you and show you where to sit.

Preschoolers and older kids will sing songs and then take part in a drama in which children put their "sins" in a paper bag. Children will watch as "Jesus" makes their "sins" disappear!

When the Treasure Time Finale Leader dismisses everyone, have children remain seated with their Clue Crew Leaders in the Treasure Time Finale area until their parents or caregivers arrive to pick them up.

Remind children to take their projects with them when they leave. Be sure to thank parents and caregivers for bringing their children to Treasure Hunt Bible Adventure.

BIBLE POINT

✺ The Bible shows us the way to live.

BIBLE BASIS

Acts 27:1-44. Paul stands firm in his faith, even in a shipwreck.

After Paul came to believe in Jesus, he fervently shared the news of Jesus everywhere he went. In Jerusalem, Paul encountered a group of men who opposed his teachings. These men incited a riot, accusing Paul of teaching false doctrine and of defiling the Temple. In the confusion of the angry mob, Paul was arrested and thrown in prison. The following years included trials, death threats, confused centurions, secret transfers to other prisons, and finally a trip to Rome where Paul could plead his case before Caesar. As if Paul hadn't encountered enough trouble, his ship ran into a violent storm and was eventually shipwrecked! Throughout the ordeal, Paul's faith remained strong. He prayed with other prisoners, encouraged his captors to be courageous, and shared his faith in God with everyone on board. Even in the worst circumstances, Paul's life reflected the power of Christ's love.

Most of the children in your VBS won't encounter the kind of persecution that Paul faced. But they'll face tough decisions, peer pressure, false religions, and secular advice that will challenge their faith. That's why it's important for kids to use God's Word as their map for life, a tool to guide them through the storms and "shipwrecks" along the way. Use today's activities to show children the power in the Bible and to help them discover its usefulness in successfully navigating life's everyday trials.

Day 5

TREASURE LAND SCHEDULE

LOCATION	ACTIVITY	MINUTES	WHAT CHILDREN WILL DO	CLASSROOM SUPPLIES	PRESCHOOL STUDENT BOOK SUPPLIES
	Treasure Hunt Sing & Play	up to 20	Sing Treasure Hunt Bible Adventure songs with older children.	Name badges	
Preschool Bible Treasure Land	Report for Adventure!	up to 10	Meet their classmates and get into their Clue Crews.	Name badges, "Bible Point" posters	
Preschool Bible Treasure Land	Bible Story Search Party	up to 15	Hear how Paul was courageous in a storm and always remembered to share God's message with others.	Bible, five inner tubes, blue bedsheet, Masonite, cereal, vacuum	
Preschool Bible Treasure Land	Rain Forest Exploration Stations	up to 25	**Option 1: Create a Storm**—Make a "storm" in a bag and remember that Paul kept his courage with God's help.	Resealable bags, spoons, blue water, dishwashing soap, fine-point permanent marker, heart-shaped beads, sand	Preschool Student Books (pp. 10-11), Spanish Gospels of John
			Option 2: Rain Forest Wrist Puppets—Make beautiful butterflies to remember they are safe in God's care.	Cuff ends of dark socks, black chenille wires, tissues, markers	
			Option 3: Block Center—Build a ship and re-enact the Bible story.	Blocks	
			Option 4: Stormy Sea Pictures—Create boats in "sea foam" and spray them with blue "sea spray."	Crayons, cotton balls, glue sticks, blue tempera paint, water, spray bottles, paper towels, paper, newsprint	
Preschool Bible Treasure Land	Chadder's Treasure Hunt Theater	up to 15	Hear how Chadder gives away his treasure and add stickers to their Bible books.	Treasure Hunt sticker sheets	
Preschool Bible Treasure Land	Treasure Treats	up to 15	Eat Sailboat Sandwiches and remember Paul's stormy journey.	Snacks provided by the Treasure Treats Leader	
	Jungle Gym Playtime Activities	up to 25	**Option 1: Shipwreck!**—Take a wildly fun ride.	Garbage can tunnel, inner tube	
			Option 2: Ping-Pong Puff—Chase Ping-Pong balls around a pool with kid-made wind.	Wading pool, water, Ping-Pong balls, straws	
			Option 3: Crocodile Swamp—Try to cross a dangerous river without getting caught by the cunning crocs!	Masking tape	
			Option 4: Free Play—Enjoy free play outdoors or in the classroom.	Playground equipment, classroom toys	
Preschool Bible Treasure Land	Sing-Along Surprise	up to 15	Sing Bible action songs.	Bible, treasure box, bubbles and bubble wand, cassette player, *Preschool Bible Treasure Land* audiocassette: "'I've Found Me a Treasure," "The B-I-B-L-E"	
	Treasure Time Finale	up to 20	Sing songs and celebrate the treasure we have in Jesus.		Spanish Gospels of John

Preschool Bible Treasure Land Prep

Before children arrive:

● Choose which Rain Forest Exploration Stations you'll use, and collect the supplies you'll need. If you choose "Tomb Tunnel," cut a large circle from the bottom of an outdoor plastic garbage can. Don't remove the whole bottom, though, because the tunnel will need the bottom rim for stability. For the "Create a Storm" option, draw a simple smiley face with a permanent marker on each of the heart beads. Also add blue food coloring to water for the activity. For "Rain Forest Wrist Puppets," cut the toes from several black socks. To create "sea spray" for the "Stormy Sea Pictures," mix blue tempera with water to create a very thin, lightly colored solution. Pour it into spray bottles.

● Choose which Jungle Gym Playtime Activities options you'll use, and collect the supplies you'll need.

● Choose which Sing-Along Surprise songs you'll use.

● Consult with the Treasure Treats Leader to find out what time the Treasure Treats Service Crew will deliver your snacks.

● Set up the ship in your Bible story area by placing five inner tubes on the floor and covering them with the sheet of Masonite used on Day 1. Have the blue sheet readily accessible.

● Arrange to have a vacuum or broom available for cleanup after Bible story.

Treasure Hunt Sing & Play
(up to 20 minutes)

Before children arrive, arrange with the Treasure Hunt Sing & Play Leader to reserve seats up front for your preschoolers.

Greet children as they arrive. Clue Crew Leaders can give children their name badges and then sit with children and involve them in this sing-along time. Preschoolers will enjoy hearing the music and doing the motions right along with the big kids!

After the Treasure Hunt Sing & Play Leader dismisses your group, have children hold hands in their Clue Crews. Travel together to your Preschool Bible Treasure Land room.

Report for Adventure!
(up to 10 minutes)

After you arrive in your room, make sure each child is wearing his or her name badge.

Blow your bamboo whistle once. Say: **Welcome to Treasure Hunt Bible Adventure! Remember my bamboo whistle? When I blow the bamboo whistle once, it means I want you to look at me.**

Blow the bamboo whistle twice. Ask:

Field Test Findings

If you choose "Create a Storm," be sure to purchase Glad resealable bags. We discovered that other brands didn't hold up as well, resulting in lots of leaks!

Day 5

● **Who remembers what two short whistle blasts mean?**

Let children respond. If most of the children were in Treasure Hunt Bible Adventure yesterday, they'll probably remember and may even assemble in their Clue Crews without further instructions.

Say: **When I blow the bamboo whistle two short times, I want you to quickly gather with your Clue Crew. Let's practice that.** Help children practice finding their crews as you blow the bamboo whistle two short times. Help new children find their assigned crews. Lead crews to the wall where you've posted the "Bible Point" posters.

✿ **BIBLE POINT**
✿ **BIBLE POINT**

Say: **Yesterday we heard that** ✿ **the Bible shows us the way to Jesus. Today we're learning that** ✿ **the Bible shows us the way to live. (Eureka!) That's very exciting because we don't have to figure everything out for ourselves. The Bible is like a map for our lives!**

To help us understand that better, let's play a fun quick game. Have half of the crews stand on one side of the room, facing the wall. Have the other half stand facing you. Pantomime "Head, Shoulders, Knees, and Toes" and silently encourage children to follow along. After a few seconds, tell the other group to turn around and face you.

Say: **OK! Now I want this group to do the motions. We'll all wait until you figure them out.** Look at children expectantly for a few seconds. Ask:

● **If I don't tell you what to do, how long do you think it will take to figure the motions out?** (Forever; a long time.)

● **What might be another way to find out what I'd like you to do?** (Ask the other group; ask you.)

Ask the first group of children to show the others what to do. Then do the motions all together several times. Say: **The Bible does the same thing for us that this group of friends did. It shows us the way to trust, to love, to pray, and it shows us the way to Jesus. Finally, today we're learning that** ✿ **the Bible shows us the way to live!** (Eureka!)

✿ **BIBLE POINT**

The Bible shows us the way to live (Eureka!) **all the time, even when our lives are very hard. Our Bible story today tells us about how one of Jesus' early followers, Paul, lived through a really hard thing. Paul was a prisoner. That means he wasn't free to go where he wanted to go or do what he wanted to do. He was trapped with some others in a ship. Some of the other prisoners were mean! Show me your mean faces. You need mean faces because you're going to be Paul's fellow prisoners. Some prisoners were probably just like Paul, who had done nothing wrong. You can choose whether to be a mean prisoner or a prisoner who had done nothing wrong. Your Clue Crew Leaders will be the prison guards who take you away into the overcrowded ship in our Bible area.**

Blow the bamboo whistle twice, and have children assemble in their Clue Crews. Have Clue Crew Leaders lead children to your story area, keeping children in a tight circle with their arms.

Bible Story Search Party

(up to 15 minutes)

As children enter the room, make a few grumbling, growling sounds, and tell the leaders to load children into the "ship," even though it's crowded.

Tell children to say "Uh-oh!" each time they hear bad news. Say: **Paul and his fellow prisoners were all loaded onto the ship. It was the wrong time of year to set sail.** (Uh-oh!) **Paul warned everyone** (cup your hands around your mouth), **"Men, I can see that this voyage is going to be disastrous!"** (Uh-oh!)

Soon the wind began to blow. Have children join you in making the sound of gusting wind. **Lightning lit up the sky!** Have a leader flash the room lights. **Waves began to crash over the sides of the ship.** Pick up the bedsheet, and wave it over and onto children's heads. **Everyone was scared, and they gave up all hope of being saved!** (Uh-oh!) **Oh, no!** Ask:

● **How do you prisoners feel now?** (Afraid; a little scared.)

Continue: **Well, those prisoners were so scared, they couldn't even eat! Paul stood up and said, "Men, you should have listened to me before this voyage began. But listen to me now!"** Whisper: **"An angel told me that not one of you will be lost. We will crash into an island, but your lives will be spared."**

Continue: **Well, the wind continued to howl, and the waves continued to push the ship around on the sea, but after two weeks, Paul said, "Men, eat up! You need your strength!"** Shake some cereal over the heads of your children, and encourage them to eat it.

"Be strong! Be brave. Remember God has said not one hair of your head will be harmed." Pick up a handful of cereal. **"Thank you, God, for this food!"** When children are done snacking, have them dust the rest of the cereal out of the boat and onto the floor to lighten the load on the ship. **"Now rest."** Encourage children to close their eyes. Pause for a quiet moment; then loudly announce: **We've hit a sandbar! The ship is sinking!** (Uh-oh!) **Swim! Swim! Swim to the island over there!** Point to the place you want children to go. When they are settled, say: **Not one hair of one prisoner's head was harmed, just as God had promised through Paul. Many people on the island trusted Paul's God. Paul had shown the people how to be courageous, and he always told them the good news God had for them, even when people didn't pay attention to him and when everyone was in danger.** (Uh-oh!) **Paul's story is found right here in the Bible** (show children Acts 27–28) **and ✪ the Bible shows us the way to live!** (Eureka!)

Say: **Let's hold hands as we get ready for our Rain Forest Exploration Stations.**

Field Test Findings

If your children are like ours, they'll be amazed by the cereal shower! They loved it, and it really focused their attention. It's a bit of a mess to clean up, but well worth it!

X

 **BIBLE POINT**

RAIN FOREST EXPLORATION STATIONS

(up to 25 minutes)

▼▼ Option 1: CREATE A STORM ▼▼▼▼▼▼▼▼▼▼▼▼

1. Give each child a resealable bag.

2. Help each child put a spoonful of sand in their bags, being careful not to let the grains get imbedded in the seal.

3. Allow each child to select a heart bead to be Paul and drop it into the bag.

4. Have the child hold the bag open while you pour blue water (about one-third of a bag) into the bag.

5. Hold the bag while the child adds a squirt of dishwashing soap. Seal the bag immediately, without letting it tip. Place this bag inside a second bag to guard against leaks.

6. Let the child shake the bag to create a storm and look for Paul. Point out ✿ the Bible shows us the way to live, no matter what is going on around us, as in Paul's story.

▼▼ Option 2: RAIN FOREST WRIST PUPPETS ▼▼▼▼

1. Give each child a sock cuff. Have them pull the cuffs up straight around their arms or legs. When the cuffs are pulled tight, you can help each child roll the cuff to form a stretchy band. Remove the bands from children's arms and legs.

2. Give each child two tissues. Let children dot the markers onto the tissues to make beautiful patterns. Discourage moving the markers around, as the tissues may tear. (The color will spread beautifully anyway!)

3. As children finish, help them twist the chenille wires around the center of the tissues to form wings.

4. Help each child push one wing and one antennae of the butterfly through the stretchy band. Then twist the chenille wire around the band to hold the wings on.

5. Show children how to put the butterflies on their wrists and "fly" them. Say: **The Bible tells us to watch the animals God created so that we can learn from them.** Remind children ✿ the Bible shows us the way to live.

RAIN FOREST EXPLORATION STATIONS

▼▼ Option 3: BLOCK CENTER ▼▼▼▼▼▼▼▼▼▼▼▼▼▼▼

1. Help children use the blocks to create a ship for multiple passengers.

2. Encourage children to act out Paul's story in their own little ship.

▼▼ Option 4: STORMY SEA PICTURES ▼▼▼▼▼▼▼▼

1. Let children each draw a ship on a sheet of paper.

2. Demonstrate how to pull apart a cotton ball so that it looks like sea foam. Then have children glue the pulled cotton around their ships.

3. Take children to a table covered with newsprint, and allow them to lightly spray the cotton with the "sea spray" in the bottles. Use paper towels to wipe the excess spray from the paper.

4. Set the papers aside to dry.

5. Encourage children to remember how God gave Paul good news to pass on to his shipmates. Ask: **How can we share good news with others?** Remind children �֍ the Bible shows us the way to live, and we can learn a lot from Paul's stories.

After about twenty-five minutes, blow your bamboo whistle once, and announce that it's time for children to clean up their Rain Forest Exploration Stations and get ready to do some more fun things.

When cleanup is complete, blow two short blasts on the bamboo whistle. Wait for children to gather with their Clue Crews, and then say: **Remember our friend Chadder Chipmunk? Yesterday he found a great treasure! Let's see what kind of adventure is in store for Chadder today on his Treasure Hunt Bible Adventure! Take hold of your friends' hands. We'll travel together to Chadder's Treasure Hunt Theater.**

Chadder's Treasure Hunt Theater

(up to 15 minutes)

Lead children to Chadder's Treasure Hunt Theater. The Chadder's Treasure Hunt Theater Leader will greet you there and show children today's portion of *Chadder's Treasure Hunt Adventure* video.

Say: **Can you believe that Chadder Chipmunk gave away his treasure? He wanted to help others, and that treasure was a big help to Captain Mike.** ✿ **The Bible shows us the way to live, too.** (Eureka!)

Let's look at our special Bible books. Have the Clue Crew Leaders distribute the Preschool Student Books. **God wanted us to know how to follow and obey him. When we're traveling, arrows show us which way to go. The Bible is God's way of telling us which way to go. To remember that, let's add these arrow stickers to the last story in our Bible books.** Have Clue Crew Leaders help each child affix the large arrow sticker to the last story in the Student Book.

✿ BIBLE POINT

ESTE EVANGELIO
DE JUAN ES
UN REGALO
DE AMOR
DE TU AMIGO(A),

Say: **Turn to your favorite story in your Bible book.** Allow children time to find their favorite stories. Ask:

● **If you wanted to hear the story about God's love, where would you turn?**

● **If you wanted to hear a story about trusting, where would you turn?**

● **If you wanted to hear a story about praying, where would you turn?**

Say: **We've also been working on Spanish Bible books too. These are special gifts to people who don't have Bibles. Now you can add a sticker to the inside cover to let your Spanish-speaking Bible partner know that this book is a special gift from you!**

Have Clue Crew Leaders help children gently detach the Spanish Bible books from the Preschool Student Books. Then have leaders help children each place a "Gift of Love" sticker onto the inside cover of the Spanish Bible books. After children have finished, say: **Let's go back to our room to have our snacks and talk more about *Chadder's Treasure Hunt Adventure*. Get into your Clue Crews and hold hands as we travel.**

Treasure Treats

(up to 15 minutes)

Return to your room, and have children sit down at tables or in another eating area. Point out that the snack looks just like a boat and can remind us of Paul's stormy adventures! Then give each child a napkin, a Sailboat Sandwich and a cup half-filled with juice. Keep a supply of paper towels handy to wipe up any spills.

As children enjoy the snack, have Clue Crew Leaders ask them what the Bible tells us about how to please God.

When children finish their snacks, have them throw away their napkins and cups. Then blow two short blasts on the bamboo whistle, and have children assemble in their Clue Crews. If you'll be going outdoors for Jungle Gym Playtime Activities, have children hold hands before you leave.

Jungle Gym Playtime Activities

(up to 25 minutes)

If you choose to go outdoors for playtime, you may want to intersperse unstructured play with some or all of the following activities. If you remain indoors, let children revisit their favorite Rain Forest Exploration Stations, or let them engage in unstructured play. (Some of the following activities may also be appropriate for your indoor area. Use your discretion when choosing safe activities for indoor Jungle Gym Playtime Activities.)

Option 1: Shipwreck!

Set an inner tube on the ground. Place the garbage can tunnel (from Day 4) on top of the tube, on its side. Choose one child to climb inside. Rock the tunnel side to side and back and forth as you review the story with this song to the tune of "Row, Row, Row Your Boat."

> **Rock, rock, rock the ship.**
> **Rock it fast and slow!**
> **Paul helped all the prisoners**
> **Who huddled down below!**
>
> **"Swim, swim, swim," he said.**
> **"Do not be afraid!**
> **God said he'd protect every**
> **Hair upon your head!"**

Gently dump your passenger out of the tunnel, and let another child have a turn.

Option 2: Ping-Pong Puff

Fill a small wading pool with water, and toss in some Ping-Pong balls. Have crews get on their knees around the pool. Then give each child a straw. Encourage each one to select a ball that he or she wants to control by blowing on it through the straw. Children will have a blast trying to direct traffic in this miniature sea storm.

Option 3: Crocodile Swamp

What rain forest expedition would be complete without an encounter with some dangerous crocs? Place two masking tape lines about ten feet apart to define your swamp. Choose a Clue Crew Leader to play the Crocodile. The Crocodile roams back and forth through the swampland with big jaws (arms) opening and closing. Teach children this rhyme:

Crocodile, Crocodile in the swamp.
Crocodile, Crocodile, please don't chomp!

As soon as children finish saying the rhyme, they must try to cross the swamp without getting caught by the croc! Whenever a child is caught, he or she becomes another crocodile in the swamp and can then catch others as they cross! Play until only one player is left.

After several rounds, ask:

● **What are some real scary things in your life?** (Storms; big dogs.)

● **Where can you go to get some ideas about how to live even when things are scary?** (My mom; the Bible.)

✵ BIBLE POINT

Remind children ✵ the Bible shows us the way to live in all kinds of situations.

Option 4: Free Play

If you're outdoors, let children play with outdoor toys such as balls or soap bubbles or use chalk on the sidewalk. Children would also enjoy outdoor playground equipment, if it's available. If you're indoors, let children play with classroom toys such as blocks, stuffed animals, or modeling dough. As children play, look for opportunities to review today's Bible Point and Bible story. Encourage them to make storm sounds by pounding with their fists, flat hands, and fingertips on some of the equipment you have set up.

After about twenty minutes, blow the bamboo whistle once to let children know it's time to finish their activities and clean up. If you're outside, blow the bamboo whistle twice after cleanup is complete to signal your return to the classroom. Then gather in the story area for singing.

Sing-Along Surprise
(up to 15 minutes)

✵ BIBLE POINT

Today's treasure is a bottle of bubbles and a bubble wand. Say:
✵ **The Bible shows us the way to live.** (Eureka!) **Today the treasure box contains something I can share with you. Here's the riddle:**

I'm lighter than air.
See me float?
You might even find me
Around a boat!

Let children guess; then show them the bubbles and blow some over their heads. After a moment of play, say: **Bubbles can disappear very quickly! But if we slow down for just a second, we can catch them!** Blow a bubble and catch it on the wand. Say: **Our week has gone by so fast, just like these bubbles. I'm going to catch a bubble for each of you, and bring it close. When I get to you, you can say one thing that you learned or that you think was really fun during this week of Treasure Hunt Bible Adventure. After you share your idea, you can reach out your finger and pop the bubble.**

Give each child a chance to share in this manner. If you have more than fifteen children, you'll want to have a helper or provide bubbles for each Clue Crew Leader to use.

Say: **I am so glad we had this chance to learn about all the things the Bible shows us the way to! The Bible shows us the way to trust!** (Eureka!) **The Bible shows us the way to love!** (Eureka!) **The Bible shows us the way to pray!** (Eureka!) **The Bible shows us the way to Jesus!** (Eureka!) **The Bible shows us the way to live!** (Eureka!) **Let's get really quiet now, and thank God for all he has shown us this week.**

Personalize this prayer time based on things your children remember.

Lead children in singing one or more of the following songs:

I've Found Me a Treasure

Chorus:

I've found me a treasure *(put hands next to mouth as if shouting and bounce from right to left with the beat);*

I've found a friend. *(Keep hands next to mouth and bounce from left to right.)*

I found Jesus *(sign "Jesus"),*

And his love will never end. *(Cross arms over chest on "love," extend right arm to side on "never," and extend left arm to side on "end.")*

I've found me a treasure *(put hands next to mouth as if shouting and bounce from right to left with the beat);*

I've found a friend. *(Keep hands next to mouth and bounce from left to right.)*

I found Jesus *(sign "Jesus"),*

And his love will never end. *(Cross arms over chest on "love," extend right arm to side on "never," and extend left arm to side on "end.")*

Day 1:

Jesus came upon a boat *(sign "Jesus")*

While walking on the sea. *(Walk in place.)*

Peter trusted in his Lord *(raise arms overhead)*

And stepped out on the Galilee. *(Walk in place.)*

(Repeat chorus)

Day 2:

Jesus taught us how to love *(sign "Jesus" and then cross arms over chest)*
In hopes that we may see *(shade eyes with hands)*
No one's greater than the next. *(Hold hands up and shake them back and forth);*
Then he washed his disciples' feet. *(Slap the bottom of one foot with the opposite hand.)*

(Repeat chorus)

Day 3:

Jesus, speaking in a garden *(put hands next to mouth),*
Showed us how to pray. *(Make prayer hands.)*
Bow your head, get on your knees *(put hands on top of head, and then pat knees)—*
Just ask it in his name. *(Raise arms overhead.)*

(Repeat chorus)

Day 4:

For God, he so loved the world *(raise arms overhead, and then cross arms over chest)*
That he gave his only Son *(sign "Jesus")*
That we may have eternal life. *(Raise arms overhead.)*
We are the chosen ones. *(Keep hands raised and shake "praise" hands with the beat.)*

(Repeat chorus)

Day 5:

Sailing in a mighty storm *(sway arms back and forth as "wind"),*
Paul's faith in God was strong. *(Flex biceps.)*
If we listen to his Word *(put hands behind ears),*
He'll show us right from wrong. *(Give thumbs-up sign on "right" and thumbs-down sign on "wrong.")*

(Repeat chorus twice)

The B–I–B–L–E

(March in place.)
The B! *(First section pumps fists overhead.)*
The I! *(Second section pumps fists overhead.)*
The B! *(Third section pumps fists overhead.)*
L-E! *(Everybody pumps fists overhead.)*

The B! *(First section pumps fists overhead.)*
The I! *(Second section pumps fists overhead.)*

The B! *(Third section pumps fists overhead.)*
L-E! *(Everybody pumps fists overhead.)*

The B-I-B-L-E *(move hands from right, to center, to left, to center),*
Yes, that's the book for me. *(Move hands from right, to center, to left, to center.)*
I stand alone on the Word of God *(move hands from right, to center, to left, to center),*
The B-I-B-L-E! *(Move hands from right, to center, to left, to center.)*

The B-I-B-L-E *(move hands from right, to center, to left, to center),*
Yes, that's the book for me. *(Move hands from right, to center, to left, to center.)*
I stand alone on the Word of God *(move hands from right, to center, to left, to center),*
The B-I-B-L-E! *(Move hands from right, to center, to left, to center.)*

Leader: **The B!** *(Leader cups hands around mouth.)*
Section 1: **The B!** *(First section pumps fists overhead.)*
Leader: **The I!** *(Leader cups hands around mouth.)*
Section 2: **The I!** *(Second section pumps fists overhead.)*
Leader: **The B!** *(Leader cups hands around mouth.)*
Section 3: **The B!** *(Third section pumps fists overhead.)*
Everyone: **L-E!** *(Everybody pumps fists overhead.)*

Leader: **The B!** *(Leader cups hands around mouth.)*
Section 1: **The B!** *(First section pumps fists overhead.)*
Leader: **The I!** *(Leader cups hands around mouth.)*
Section 2: **The I!** *(Second section pumps fists overhead.)*
Leader: **The B!** *(Leader cups hands around mouth.)*
Section 3: **The B!** *(Third section pumps fists overhead.)*
Everyone: **L-E!** *(Everybody pumps fists overhead.)*

The B-I-B-L-E *(move hands from right, to center, to left, to center),*
Yes, that's the book for me. *(Move hands from right, to center, to left, to center.)*
I stand alone on the Word of God *(move hands from right, to center, to left, to center),*
The B-I-B-L-E! *(Move hands from right, to center, to left, to center.)*

The B-I-B-L-E *(move hands from right, to center, to left, to center),*
Yes, that's the book for me. *(Move hands from right, to center, to left, to center.)*
I stand alone on the Word of God *(move hands from right, to center, to left, to center),*
I stand alone on the Word of God *(march in place),*
I stand alone on the Word of God *(march in place),*
The B-I-B-L-E! *(Punch fists out and up gradually, ending with palms open.)*

Have children stand and sing this song to the tune of "Here We Go 'Round the Mulberry Bush."

The Bible shows us the way to live,
Way to live, way to live.
The Bible shows us the way to live
As children of God.

Have children think of ways that God would have them live. As each child mentions something, have the whole group affirm the idea by singing the song again. You may wish to ad-lib and act out some of the children's ideas.

After the last song, have Clue Crew Leaders collect any projects children have completed, as well as the Spanish Gospels of John. Then blow two short blasts on the bamboo whistle, and have children assemble in their Clue Crews. Have children hold hands before they leave your room.

Treasure Time Finale
(up to 20 minutes)

Lead children to the room you are using for Treasure Time Finale. The Treasure Time Finale Leader will greet you and show you where to sit.

Preschoolers and older kids will sing songs and then bring their Spanish Bible books forward as a special offering, sharing this treasure with people around the world.

When the Treasure Time Finale Leader dismisses everyone, have children remain seated with their Clue Crew Leaders in the Treasure Time Finale area until their parents or caregivers arrive to pick them up.

Remind children to take their projects and their Treasure Hunt Adventure Student Books with them when they leave. Be sure to thank parents and caregivers for bringing their children to Treasure Hunt Bible Adventure.

Song Lyrics Sheet

THE B-I-B-L-E

The B!
The I!
The B!
L-E!
The B!
The I!
The B!
L-E!

The B-I-B-L-E, yes, that's the book
for me.
I stand alone on the Word of God,
the B-I-B-L-E!

The B-I-B-L-E, yes, that's the book
for me.
I stand alone on the Word of God,
the B-I-B-L-E!

The B! (The B!)
The I! (The I!)
The B! (The B!)
L-E! (L-E!)
The B! (The B!)
The I! (The I!)
The B! (The B!)
L-E! (L-E!)

The B-I-B-L-E, yes, that's the book
for me.
I stand alone on the Word of God,
the B-I-B-L-E!

The B-I-B-L-E, yes, that's the book
for me.
I stand alone on the Word of God,
I stand alone on the Word of God,
I stand alone on the Word of God,
the B-I-B-L-E!

HE'S GOT THE WHOLE
WORLD IN HIS HANDS

He's got the whole world in his hands.
He's got the whole world in his hands.
He's got the whole world in his hands.
He's got the whole world in his hands.

He's got the wind and the rain in his hands.
He's got the wind and the rain in his hands.
He's got the wind and the rain in his hands.
He's got the whole world in his hands.

He's got everybody here in his hands.
He's got everybody here in his hands.
He's got everybody here in his hands.
He's got the whole world in his hands.

Song Lyrics Sheet
I'VE FOUND ME A TREASURE

Chorus:

I've found me a treasure;
I've found a friend.
I found Jesus,
And his love will never end.
I've found me a treasure;
I've found a friend.
I found Jesus,
And his love will never end.

Day 1:

Jesus came upon a boat
While walking on the sea.
Peter trusted in his Lord
And stepped out on the Galilee.

(Repeat chorus)

Day 2:

Jesus taught us how to love
In hopes that we may see
No one's greater than the next.
Then he washed his disciples' feet.

(Repeat chorus)

Day 3:

Jesus, speaking in a garden,
Showed us how to pray.
Bow your head, get on your knees—
Just ask it in his name.

(Repeat chorus)

Day 4:

For God, he so loved the world
That he gave his only Son
That we may have eternal life.
We are the chosen ones.

(Repeat chorus)

Day 5:

Sailing in a mighty storm,
Paul's faith in God was strong.
If we listen to his Word,
He'll show us right from wrong.

(Repeat chorus twice)

JESUS LOVES ME

Jesus loves me! This I know,
For the Bible tells me so.
Little ones to him belong;
They are weak, but he is strong.

Yes, Jesus loves me!
Yes, Jesus loves me!
Yes, Jesus loves me!
The Bible tells me so.

Jesus loves me! He will stay
Close beside me all the way.
If I love him, when I die,
He will take me home on high.

Yes, Jesus loves me!
Yes, Jesus loves me!
Yes, Jesus loves me!
The Bible tells me so.

Jesus loves me! This I know,
For the Bible tells me so.
Little ones to him belong;
They are weak, but he is strong.

Yes, Jesus loves me!
Yes, Jesus loves me!
Yes, Jesus loves me!
The Bible tells me so.

Yes, Jesus loves me!
Yes, Jesus loves me!
Yes, Jesus loves me!
The Bible tells me so.

TEACH YOUR PRESCHOOLERS AS JESUS TAUGHT WITH GROUP'S *HANDS-ON BIBLE CURRICULUM*™

Hands-On Bible Curriculum™ **for preschoolers** helps your preschoolers learn the way they learn best—by touching, exploring, and discovering. With active and authentic learning, preschoolers love learning about the Bible, and they really remember what they learn.

Because small children learn best through repetition, Preschoolers and Pre-K & K will learn one important point per lesson, and Toddlers & 2s will learn one point each month with **Hands-On Bible Curriculum**. These important lessons will stick with them and comfort them during their daily lives. Your children will learn God is our friend, who Jesus is, and we can always trust Jesus.

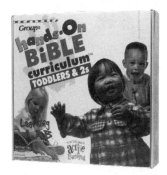  

The **Learning Lab**® is packed with age-appropriate learning tools for fun, faith-building lessons. Toddlers & 2s explore big **Interactive StoryBoards**™ with enticing textures that toddlers love to touch— like sandpaper for earth, cotton for clouds, and blue cellophane for water. While they hear the Bible story, children also *touch* the Bible story. And they learn. **Bible Big Books**™ captivate Preschoolers and Pre-K & K while teaching them important Bible lessons. With **Jumbo Bible Puzzles**™ and involving **Learning Mats**™, your children will see, touch, and explore their Bible stories. Each quarter there's a brand new collection of supplies to keep your lessons fresh and involving.

Just order one **Learning Lab** and one **Teacher Guide** for each age level, add a few common classroom supplies, and presto—you have everything you need to inspire and build faith in your children. For more interactive fun, introduce your children to the age-appropriate puppet (Cuddles the Lamb, Whiskers the Mouse, or Pockets the Kangaroo) who will be your teaching assistant and their friend. No student books are required!

Hands-On Bible Curriculum is also available for elementary grades.

Order today from your local Christian bookstore, or write: Group Publishing, P.O. Box 485, Loveland, CO 80539.

BRING THE BIBLE TO LIFE FOR YOUR 1ST- THROUGH 6TH-GRADERS... WITH GROUP'S HANDS-ON BIBLE CURRICULUM™

Energize your kids with Authentic Learning!

In each lesson, students will participate in exciting and memorable learning experiences using fascinating gadgets and gizmos. Your elementary students will discover biblical truths and <u>remember</u> what they learn because they're <u>doing</u> instead of just listening.

You'll save time and money too!

Simply follow the quick and easy instructions in the **Teacher Guide**. You'll get tons of material for an energy-packed 35- to 60- minute lesson. Plus, you'll SAVE BIG over other curriculum programs that require you to buy expensive separate student books—all student handouts in Group's **Hands-On Bible Curriculum** are photocopiable!

In addition to the easy-to-use **Teacher Guide**, you'll get all the essential teaching materials you need in a ready-to-use **Learning Lab**®. No more running from store to store hunting for lesson materials—all the active-learning tools you need to teach 13 exciting Bible lessons to any size class are provided for you in the **Learning Lab**.

Challenging topics each quarter keep your kids coming back!

Group's **Hands-On Bible Curriculum** covers topics that matter to your kids and teaches them the Bible with integrity. Switching topics every month keeps your 1st- through 6th-graders enthused and coming back for more. The full two-year program will help your kids make God-pleasing decisions...recognize their God-given potential...and seek to grow as Christians.

Take the boredom out of Sunday school, children's church, and midweek meetings for your elementary students. Make your job easier and more rewarding with no-fail lessons that are ready in a flash. Order Group's **Hands-On Bible Curriculum** for your 1st- through 6th-graders today. (Also available for Toddlers & 2s, Preschool, and Pre-K and K!)